Fashion Accessories
Since 1500

Fashion

Accessories

Since 1500

GEOFFREY WARREN

UNWIN HYMAN
London Sydney

DRAMA BOOK PUBLISHERS
New York

For my twin brother Roger

Acknowledgements

My thanks are due to my twin brother Roger for his valuable comments, to my editor Emma Callery, to Elizabeth Brooke-Smith of Unwin Hyman and to my agent Mrs Doreen Montgomery for their support and enthusiasm throughout a long task. I would also like to thank Mr Alex Kroll and Ms Sian Dalziel for permission to consult and use *Vogue*'s library.

First published in Great Britain by Unwin Hyman an imprint of Unwin Hyman Limited, 1987.

UNWIN HYMAN
Denmark House, 37–39 Queen Elizabeth Street, London SE1 2QB
and
40 Museum Street, London WC1A 1LU

Allen & Unwin (Australia) Ltd
8 Napier Street, North Sydney, NSW 2060, Australia

Allen & Unwin New Zealand Ltd with the Port Nicholson Press
60 Cambridge Terrace, Wellington, New Zealand

DRAMA BOOK PUBLISHERS
PO Box 816, Gracie Station, New York, New York 10028

ISBN 0 7135 2682 3 (UK edition)
ISBN 0-89676-094-4 (US edition)

British Library Cataloguing in Publication Data
(UK edition only)
Warren, Geoffrey
    Fashion accessories: 1500–1970.
    1. Dress accessories —— History
    I. Title
    391'.44'0903   GT2050

Designed by Geoffrey Warren and Norman Reynolds
Typeset by Cambridge Photosetting Services
Printed and bound in Great Britain at The Bath Press, Avon

Contents

Introduction

FASHION ACCESSORIES can, of course, be purely practical: headwear, shoes and gloves to keep one dry and warm; belts to hold up trousers and skirts; pouches, purses and handbags for money; umbrellas and parasols to keep off rain or sun. But they can be so much more. They are worn or carried to be 'in fashion'; out of vanity; to attract the opposite sex – or to make one's own sex envious.

More often than clothes, accessories can proclaim the wearer's wealth, rank or status in society. For instance, 16th-century embroidered gloves and lace-edged handkerchieves were more usually held than carried – mere status symbols. In the 16th century, a man's black velvet 'Court' bonnet gave him immediate courtly distinction. 'Real' jewellery in any age, denotes some wealth but this was even more evident from 1500 to the late 18th century when jewels were not only sewn on to garments but on to all kinds of accessories. Only the rich carried silver-topped canes, jewelled snuff boxes or the most exotic fans. Only they wore diamond-studded shoe buckles or carried the frothiest of parasols. Only the *outré* woman would deck her towering powdered wig with feathers, flowers and even a miniature ship, and only dashing Regency bucks would jingle their fob seals as they sauntered in their beautifully made Hessian boots. To distinguish themselves from their servants, early Victorian women and girls of the rising,

wealthy middle-class, wore short white or lemon-coloured kid gloves indoors to show that they did no work. The early Victorian gentleman displayed his male superiority by wearing a tall stove-pipe top hat; his womenfolk their female inferiority in their face-concealing bonnets.

Furthermore, accessories can symbolize an age: the Elizabethan ruff; the 'Cavalier' lace collar; the Gainsborough 'picture' hat; the Victorian bonnet; the Edwardian wing-collar; the 'My Fair Lady' hat; the 1920's cloche; 1930's brogues and the 1960's women's long boot. From the end of the 18th century, accessories, especially for women, changed more rapidly than clothes. A woman might have only a relatively small number of clothes to choose from – but a multitude of handbags and shoes.

The depiction of the most accurate of costumes can be spoiled by the wrong accessories – or those incorrectly made or badly proportioned. In this book, therefore, I have set out to illustrate and describe the wide range of accessories which are appropriate and fashionable at given periods. To aid the important all-over picture, each period is illustrated with a full-length figure wearing the kind of garments with which the accessories would have been worn or carried, together with a brief summing-up of the fashion trend. In the main, the book deals with the fashionable, upper-classes. The middle or 'merchant' class is included only when its clothes and accessories sharply differed. After the late 18th century, the less well-off tended to wear garments and accessories similar to those of the wealthy. In America, except for the early Settlers' Puritan garb and what was worn in the Wild West period, fashion on the whole, closely followed that of Europe. However, until the 19th century, it was usually less extravagant and exaggerated.

As well as consulting recent and contemporary costume books, journals, magazines and fashion plates I have also made use of books devoted to portrait painters. Among the 'greats' are Holbein, Kneller, Gainsborough and Reynolds; among the lesser-known, but equally valuable, are Hans Eworth, Marcus

Gheeraerts and Cornelius Johnson. Such miniaturists as Nicholas Hilliard, Isaac Oliver and Samuel Cooper are particularly useful regarding head-dresses, hats, ruffs, collars and jewellery. The Victoria and Albert Museum, The Tate and The National Portrait Galleries, among others, have held many exhibitions of portrait painters and miniaturists and I have found their illustrated catalogues of immense help. Reproductions of portraits can also be found in likely and unlikely places: such as illustrated biographies and histories; in magazines devoted to the arts and antiques, in general magazines, in Colour Supplements and even newspapers. For those making a serious study of fashion it is a good idea to keep files or scrapbooks.

1500–1525

In the early years of the century, men's fashion was strongly influenced by Italian and Franco-Flemish styles.

Shirts were low-necked and often voluminous; doublets and jerkins tight-fitting, the front opening filled-in with a stomacher. Men wore short, medium or long coats, gowns, cassocks or cloaks, which were fur-lined, with wide, thrown-back collars. Hair – except in Germany – was worn long. The Milan bonnet worn here, was almost universal.

By the 1520s, doublets were more elaborate and slashing – of German-Swiss origin – was universally applied to garments and accessories. Shoulders wide; shoes broad-toed.

In an unhygenic age, the wealthy protected themselves with perfume and musk contained in pomanders; often of gold filigree and richly jewelled and enamelled. Men carried them on chains; women at the end of long girdles.

Apart from gauntlets worn for hunting, gloves were short with tabbed cuffs. Made of leather, silk or velvet, they were often slashed at the knuckles to reveal rings. Also worn by women.

Shoes were broad-toed, plain or slashed; slipper styles were often fastened by straps or ribbons over the instep. They were made of leather, velvet or silk, with leather or cork soles; and heels were rare until the 1580s.

Boots were worn mostly for riding or travelling. They were made of leather with tops turned down to show a coloured lining; frequently slashed at the ankles. Pouches, of soft leather or velvet, often on metal frames, were decorated with cord and tassels. A dagger could be slotted behind.

1. Feathered black felt hat worn over a caul. Cauls were made of rich materials or gold or silver network. (Cauls and coifs were the only male headwear permitted in the presence of royalty.) 2. Slashed leather ornamented with aiglets. 3. Brown velvet bonnet looped up and tied; brooches were pinned to most headwear. 4. Caul or turban of striped silk and cord; principally worn in Italy. 5. Loop-brimmed bonnet over a caul.

1500–1525

English, French and Flemish

During this period, fashion was still medieval. Skirts were very long and sleeves wide and furlined with narrower undersleeves, or narrow from shoulder to wrist, terminating in deep cuffs. *Décolletage* was square. Girdles were hung with a medallion, cross, pomander or book.

1

2

All head-dresses, usually of black velvet, were based on the old medieval hood and covered the head and shoulders. By the beginning of the 16th century, such hoods were elaborated in various ways. **1.** A Flemish version, split at the sides, its front lappets embroidered and jewelled. It was thrown back to reveal a contrasting, red, lining, a jewelled band and a frill of gold gauze. **2.** The French hood had a front curve of white satin trimmed with pearls. **3.** and *full-length*: The Pediment, or gable, head-dress, worn only in England. After about 1520 the rich fabric side lappets were turned up over the stiffened and jewelled 'gable' and the hair was concealed by striped silk rolls. Huge pendants on thin necklaces were common to all three countries, as were elaborate girdles of leather and gilded metal.

3

German

Dress varied in a number of small States but the principal fashion was for tight-waisted dresses with heavily pleated skirts and narrow sleeves. Low necklines were filled-in with necklaces and chains finished with elaborate pendants.

1. The balloon head-dress made of padded and embroidered linen with a gauze veil, was a purely German fashion. **2.** Mannish hats, worn over cauls at a rakish angle, were decorated with feathers and jewels.

Italian

Dresses were full, soft and flowing with high waists, very low *décolletage* and immense sleeves pinned with brooches.

Long or frizzed hair was worn with large 'halo' hats, turbans of puffed and jewelled silk or small round caps with snoods – all principally Italian styles. Jewellery mainly consisted of simple necklaces and bracelets.

1500–1525

With changes in the social order, a new middle-class emerged: merchants, burghers and minor gentry, among whom wealth counted more than lineage. This class wore modified versions of the clothes of their 'betters', with some garments and accessories peculiar to them. The chief male garment was the fur-lined gown, with hanging sleeves, the origin of today's mayoral gown.

Headwear was comparatively simple. Full length. Most popular was the small turned-up, brimmed bonnet with a small medallion. **1.** and **2.** Wide-brimmed hats were worn at an angle by the smart or straight by the elderly, over a coif which tied under the chin. **3.** Floppy, tam'o shanter-style berets were popular in Germany.

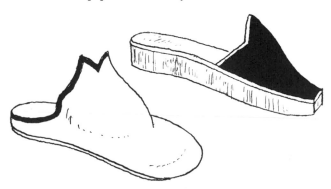

Belts carried one large pouch or a number of items: purse, knife, ink-well, sand for drying ink, etc.

Shoes were round-toed and often slipper-like. Thick-soled over-shoes were worn in bad weather.

Middle-class women aped higher-born ladies but were more inclined to fill-in their necklines with pleated chemises. In general the middle-class dressed at least ten years out-of-date; among the elderly, this holds good in all classes.

Middle-class women often pinned up their skirts to facilitate movement. Girdles were low-slung. **1.** Bags, purses and a knife, suspended on a cord. **2.** Tooled leather with a gilded metal trefoil clasp and 'drop' ending in a tassel. **3.** A long leather belt with elaborate tongue, worn *at the back*; a particularly German fashion. **4.** and *full-length*: Flemish women wore the *béguin* made of stiffened linen, lawn or cambric. **5.** English women wore versions of the gable or, **6.** the 'lettice' cap – lettice was a rabbit-like fur. This cap was also made of black velvet and worn until the 1570s.

1525–1550

German fashion predominated. It was an ultra-masculine look: wide-shouldered and bulky, making men stand with legs apart. Shirts were beautifully embroidered; slashed doublets worn under long-skirted jerkins; slops finished just above the knees; the codpiece was almost universal. Some outfits were entirely in silk and satin, as here, but it was a period of rich, often embroidered, velvet, or fur, and gilded and jewelled ornaments.

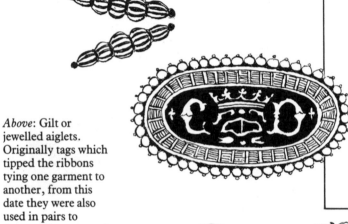

Above: Gilt or jewelled aiglets. Originally tags which tipped the ribbons tying one garment to another, from this date they were also used in pairs to decorate bonnets and hats. *Right:* A typical gold, enamelled and pearl-edged medallion (also called an enseigne or ouch), which was pinned to headwear.

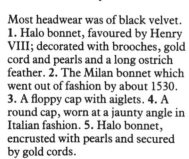

Most headwear was of black velvet.
1. Halo bonnet, favoured by Henry VIII; decorated with brooches, gold cord and pearls and a long ostrich feather. **2.** The Milan bonnet which went out of fashion by about 1530. **3.** A floppy cap with aiglets. **4.** A round cap, worn at a jaunty angle in Italian fashion. **5.** Halo bonnet, encrusted with pearls and secured by gold cords.

2

3

4

1

5

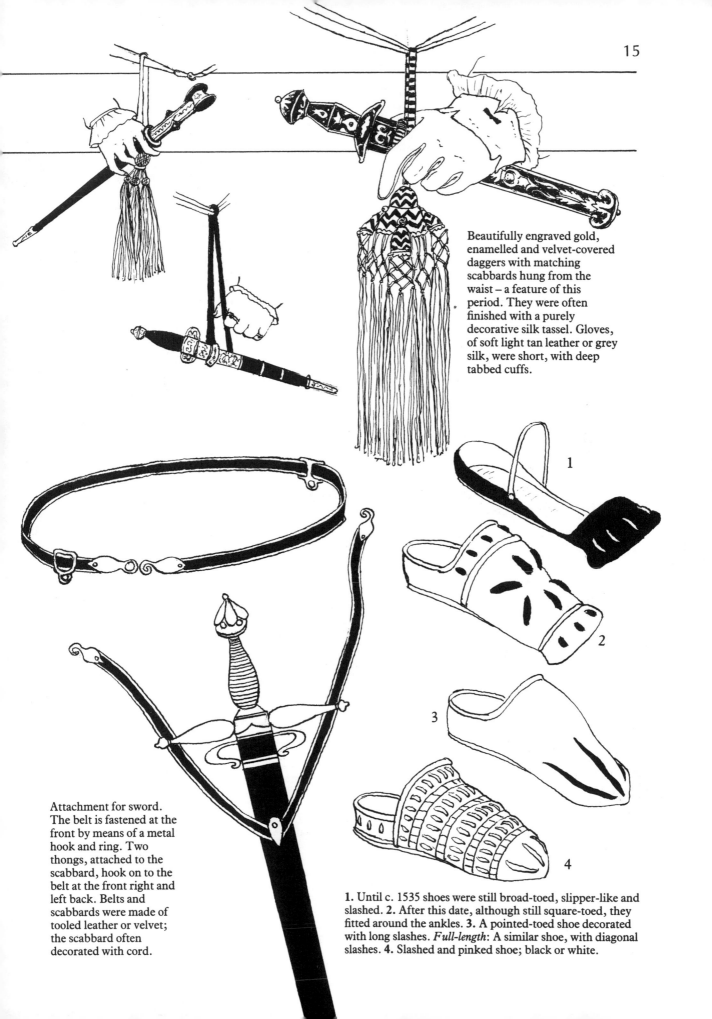

Beautifully engraved gold, enamelled and velvet-covered daggers with matching scabbards hung from the waist – a feature of this period. They were often finished with a purely decorative silk tassel. Gloves, of soft light tan leather or grey silk, were short, with deep tabbed cuffs.

Attachment for sword. The belt is fastened at the front by means of a metal hook and ring. Two thongs, attached to the scabbard, hook on to the belt at the front right and left back. Belts and scabbards were made of tooled leather or velvet; the scabbard often decorated with cord.

1. Until c. 1535 shoes were still broad-toed, slipper-like and slashed. 2. After this date, although still square-toed, they fitted around the ankles. 3. A pointed-toed shoe decorated with long slashes. *Full-length*: A similar shoe, with diagonal slashes. 4. Slashed and pinked shoe; black or white.

1525–1550

English and French

The woman in the foreground wears an elaboration of the previous English style and a smaller gable head-dress; one side of the fall pinned up. The French woman (*behind*) is wearing a French hood and she also features a new dress with its yoke, collar and bishop's sleeves.

1. German-style man's bonnet, trimmed with aiglets and an ouch, worn over a white pearl-edged cap and a pleat of gold gauze. **2.** A French hood with a snood made of green velvet and gold braid, decorated with brooches. **3.** English version of the French hood, with jewelled upper and lower billaments; ties under the chin and with a black velvet fall. **4.** Aiglet and brooch-decorated halo bonnet worn over a small caul with a jewelled pendant; drop earrings.

Because of long skirts, women's shoes were rarely in evidence. However, it is important to know that they closely resembled those of the men, *never* heeled and either round or square-toed.

German

Natural waists were tightly corsetted; sleeves a series of puffs; skirts barrel-like; *décolletage* bare or a collared chemise was worn; many chains.

Men's hats, topped with feathers, were still popular, as were heavily jewelled hoods covered with stiffened gauze over-caps, turned up at the corners.

Italian

High-waisted, ample skirts; full, puffed sleeves; low neck-lines, edged with frilled chemise or patterned silk scarves. Ornamental aprons were also fashionable.

Heads were bound with plaited hair or covered in huge, soft or firm silk, or braided and jewelled turbans caught with brooches.

1550–1560

Although Italian doublets with deep skirts and puffed sleeves were fashionable at the English Court, Spanish dress, seen here, began its 60 year sway over the whole of Europe. Doublets were low-waisted; trunk-hose moderately full; gowns short and full with bulbous sleeves.

1

2

Full-length: The small Spanish, or Court, bonnet, usually of black velvet with a jewelled band and feather would be the 'correct' wear for the rest of the century. During this decade alternatives included, **1.** the English bonnet which had a stiff crown and brim and, **2.** the French hat resembling a 19th-century bowler. The frill of the skirt which appeared over the top of the doublet was the germ of the ruff to come. In France, little turn-down collars were in vogue.

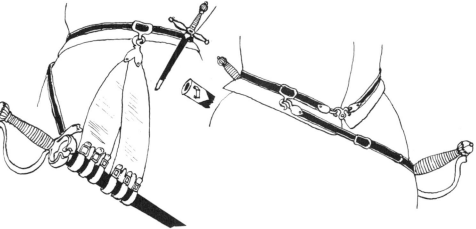

A more complicated method of carrying the sword made its appearance now. The belt – curved to fit the waistline – fastened with a metal ring and hooks. A thong, attached to the scabbard, hooked on to the belt on the right. The scabbard was further held by the hangers or carriage which hooked on to the back. The dagger scabbard slotted into the belt. *Left*: shoe with high tongue and ribbon tie.

Front: Dresses combining the 1520s–1540s sleeves and the patterned underskirt, with the yoke and collar, were worn over the bell shaped Spanish farthingale: a framework of hoops. *Behind*: An alternative, of Spanish origin dating from c.1550, was the narrow gown, with puffed sleeves. It was left open or fastened with jewels or ribbons from neck to hem.

Gloves were short and made of dark tan leather with light cuffs or, as here, of pale leather or silk, studded with pearls. Huge pendants were still the main form of jewellery. *Left*: The Holy Monogram 'IHS', made from gold and jewels, with pearl drops.

1. Stiff German-style, jewelled hat worn over a gold and pearl caul, hair dressed in 'bangs'; note the small ruff.
2. French, caul-like head-dress, worn at the back of the head. 3. Square-shaped French hood popular in England, worn with black velvet curve; note the important necklace and pendant. 4. Simple curved French hood, made of black velvet edged with white silk.

1560–1570

The doublet was still easy-fitting with a very shallow, scalloped shirt, as in this English version. The alternative was long-skirted, as worn by the Frenchman on the facing page. Stripes were a feature of this decade achieved by braid or bands of embroidered material called guards. Short, sleeved cloaks and full, collarless capes were equally fashionable.

For the rest of the century, men wore oval pendants (crosses in Catholic countries) or gold and enamelled miniature-cases. A wife's or mistress's ring was also threaded on a ribbon or sash.

1

2

3

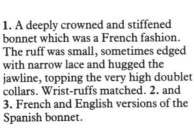

1. A deeply crowned and stiffened bonnet which was a French fashion. The ruff was small, sometimes edged with narrow lace and hugged the jawline, topping the very high doublet collars. Wrist-ruffs matched. 2. and 3. French and English versions of the Spanish bonnet.

Skin-tight boots, fastened by buttons on the outside leg, were made of very soft leather and often attached by two straps under the trunk hose. Shoes were easy-fitting, swelling slightly across the toes. Most were razed – ornamented with large or small slashes and/or stitching. They always matched the hose at this date: dark with dark, light with light.

Pouches, to hold a small linen or cambric handkerchief and money, were of two kinds. **1.** Bulbous black velvet pouch on a small frame, decorated with braid and beads. **2.** A gilded metal frame holds the shape of this half-moon, black velvet pouch; a tassel was optional.

1560–1570

The 'high-bodied' gown was in fashion until the late 1560s; note the vestigial hanging sleeves. A concurrent fashion, dating from c.1565, is seen opposite: *décolletage* filled-in with a partlet; narrow sleeves much braided and puffed; very full, gathered skirts. Both fashions were worn over a farthingale and much bedecked with necklaces and chains.

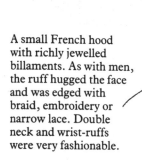

Jewelled and enamelled aiglets were often liberally scattered over the gown. *Left*: the 'flea-fur', first seen on page 17, was the skin of a whole sable or martin, with gilded and jewelled muzzle and paws. It was fastened to the waist by a chain and worn over one shoulder or carried in the hand. An Italian and English fashion only.

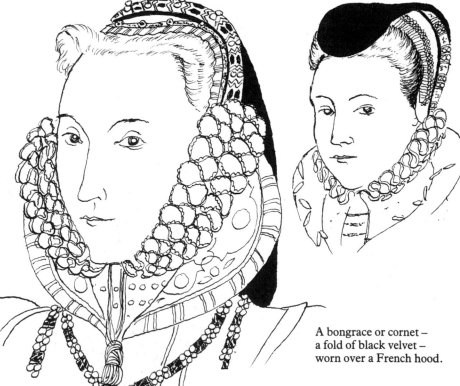

A small French hood with richly jewelled billaments. As with men, the ruff hugged the face and was edged with braid, embroidery or narrow lace. Double neck and wrist-ruffs were very fashionable.

A bongrace or cornet – a fold of black velvet – worn over a French hood.

Small wrist-ruffs – to match the neck-ruff – were often edged with chequered braid. Elaborate girdles sported huge medallions: here, a Roman cameo set in gold. Gloves were short: of dark tan leather with lighter cuffs – plain or scalloped, with or without buttons.

1

2

3

All these head-dresses were worn with both styles of dress.
1. French hood with puffs of silk; pendant on chain. 2. Small velvet hat and caul trimmed with large white beads. 3. Small red velvet bonnet decorated with brooches and red and white feathers. Note the white enamel star-shaped hair ornament stuck into frizzed hair.

1570–1580

Typical Spanish dress – *de rigueur* from Portugal to Poland. The doublet was smooth-fitting, often padded and boned and slightly peascod-bellied – protruding over the stomach. Trunk-hose, full and stuffed, with narrow panes. Cape short and full, decorated with braid, embroidery or pearls. It was an elegant, haughty-looking style.

Shoes rose higher over the instep and were slashed and stitched in a number of ways. Heels, *left*, were still rare, mainly in France.

The Spanish bonnet was still fashionable but a full, high hat, first seen in Italy in the late 1560s, soon became a popular rival. Made of velvet or silk and lined with buckram it was pleated into a narrow brim; the join concealed by a jewelled band or twist of material. The ultra-fashionable young man wore it at a rakish angle.

In the middle-class, a rich merchant wore a heavily-patterned gown, bound with velvet and lined with fur; beneath it he would wear less-exaggerated, upper-class clothes. His wife would wear old-fashioned hanging sleeves and covered bodice (although square chemise-filled *décolletage* was also in style) and a small muff on a chain.

1

2

3

4

5

Small white caps, once fashionable in the 1550s, were much worn by women. **1.** They would also wear a wide hat with ribbons, over a coif.
2. Men's hats were popular too. **3.** Woman's velvet pouch with metal clasp, hung on cords.

Although a number of men wore small bonnets, hats of all kinds were much in favour.
4. An elderly man would wear a wide-brimmed felt hat with a hard crown, over a coif.
5. Young men preferred copotain hats swathed with cloth, rather than the rich man's jewelled band.

1570–1580

English

This decade is typified by wide skirts, enormous shoulder wings, larger ruffs, embroidered partlets and bosoms smothered in necklaces and chains.

Wrist-ruffs were often worn with a lace cuff. Short, dark tan gloves were given embroidered, and often jewelled cuffs. Rigid fans consisted of white or coloured ostrich feathers mounted on elaborately jewelled gold or silver handles. They were carried or hung from the waist by a cord or ribbon.

1. A little girl would wear a lawn cap with a jewelled band and a small embroidered collar. **2.** A deep French hood of heavy gold mesh, puffs and brooches. **3.** High, hard hats were fashionable; jewelled bands, a cluster of white and coloured feathers; worn over sumptuous cauls.

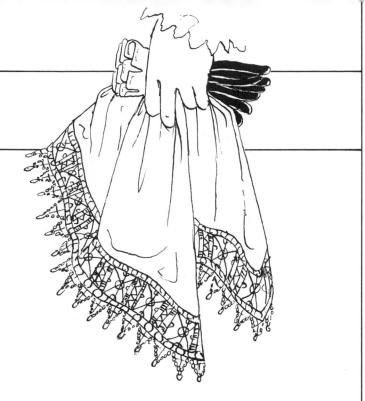

Spanish

Spanish women were exceptionally elegant: still favouring the closed gown: the long line emphasized by rich braid and jewels.

As a status symbol most upper-class European women carried large cambric or silk handkerchiefs edged with white, gold or silver lace.

Although these examples of headwear are Spanish, they were also worn in most of Europe. **1.** The figure-of-eight, lace-edged head-dress echoes the ruff. **2.** A starched transparent cap worn over a network caul. **3.** A man's Court bonnet over a pearl-encrusted caul. **4.** A very Spanish man's hat, superbly decorated with huge (probably imitation) pearls, brooches and ostrich feathers.

1580–1590

The peascod-bellied doublet was at its most grotesque, trunk hose at their briefest – a mere roll around the hips – and the ruff at its greatest size. Fashion was at its most fussy: differently patterned doublet, trunk-hose, canions, cloak and stockings. Fashion was more elegant (*facing page*) in its French-inspired form.

Richly corded, black velvet pouch on a metal frame.

1. High-crowned, felt hat with cypress band, jewel, ostrich tips and osprey feather. 'Cartwheel' ruffs were plain or edged with deep lace.
2. Undecorated hat. Collars or falling-bands were a new fashion – here, embroidered and lace-edged.
3. 'Cabbage' ruff or ruff *á la confusion*. *Facing page*: Hard hat with pearl band and feather; matching falling-band and cuff.

Cross-garters (worn by Malvolio in *Twelfth Night*) were a particularly English, German and Flemish fashion. The garter was placed below the knee in front, twisted cross-wise at the back and brought forward above the knee and tied in a bow at the front or side. Worn with trunk hose, canions or tight Venetians.

1. High-tongued, white silk shoe, ornamented with stitching. **2.** The first appearance of a heel in England: on a white silk shoe. **3.** An overshoe or pantofle, made of black velvet or leather and worn in bad weather. 1 and 3 can be seen worn by the full-length figure on the facing page; velvet pantofle for indoors.

1580–1590

Skirts reached their greatest circumference; sleeves their fullest and ruffs their deepest; so deep in France that women had to use long-handled spoons in order to eat. Cuffs were often worn in preference to the old wrist-ruff; looped chains were still worn, but by the end of the decade they were replaced by long ropes of pearls.

Huge, phantasmagoric pendants of gold, jewels, enamel and pearls, were in vogue from the 1570s to the 1590s; worn on the bosom or pinned to sleevees.

1

2

3

1. A pearl-edged cap topped by a jewelled and feathered bat. **2.** The white linen and lace heart-shaped 'Mary Queen of Scots' hood appeared in the late 1570s, influencing head-dresses until 1620. **3.** Another style of cap. Hair was dressed to fit the cap shape and stuck with jewels; these were also pinned to ruffs.

1590–1600

In general, clothes were softer. Doublets with only small peascod-bellies had wings and skirts divided into deep tassets. Stripes and dot patterns were in favour as were canions (illustrated), made of plaited braid. Hair was long, sometimes with a love-lock. Moustaches were in vogue.

Shoes, light coloured or black, were almost universally tied in a bow over the instep. Skin-tight boots were worn with boot-hose to prevent damage to the silk stockings beneath; the lace tops often pulled up to show. *Left*: Tan gloves, white cuffs trimmed with bows.

High-crowned and, usually, wide-brimmed black hats were all the rage – especially among the young intelligensia. Falling-bands were replacing ruffs but the young sometimes wore loosely set ruffs which did not fit the jaw-line. A small ruff over a starched lawn falling-band was also fashionable.

1590–1600

The French, or drum, farthingale – a series of concentric hoops – appeared in the late 1580s and dominated the 1590s and early 17th century. Waists were deep and pointed; shoulders high and wide and the open, or fan, ruff more usual than the closed. Patterned sleeves and stomacher matched, with either a plain gown (illustrated) or an exposed, patterned petticoat.

Muffs were of fur or fur covered with material; here, orange velvet embroidered with pearls.

The rigid fan continued to be in favour until the 1620s, but the folding fan, originating in the East and made fashionable in France by Catherine de Medici in the 1560s was not seen in England until the late 1580s. It was embroidered or painted and often edged with pearls.

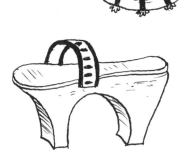

With shorter skirts, shoes became important for the first time. Usually made of white silk, they were pinked, embroidered or decorated with jewels and pearls and had thick, cork soles. *Left*: two chopines: 'platform' overshoes, worn in bad weather. The taller was worn principally in Venice.

1. So-called mitten, in fact a glove with no fingers; black velvet and leather, both embroidered. 2. Fine leather, embroidered with silks and sequins and edged with metal lace. 3. Braided cuffs trimmed with gold-bead tassels. 4. Braided, jewelled and fringed cuff. Jewel pinned to wrist-ruff.

5. Elaborate diadem-like head-dresses were fashionable especially at Court: exquisite concoctions of wired pearls, sequins and, often, feathers. Hair was dressed high over pads (or wigs were worn) and could be stuck with pearls and gems. 6. Black felt hat worn over lace-edged cap; also favoured by the middle-class and minor gentry. 7. Superb stiffened black gauze and black lace-edged head-dress; note the fashion for side curls.

1600–1610

The doublet was still cut on the same lines. Although short trunk hose, with or without canions, were worn, full trunk hose, Venetians, breeches, slops or galligaskins (synonymous terms for the same garment) were more fashionable. These, together with ample cloaks, gave a bulky appearance – offset by diverse hats and neckwear.

Nightcap of embroidered linen with metal lace trim; worn with night-gown (like the modern dressing-gown) and generally indoors, especially by older men.

Shoes still fastened over a high tongue but were more decorated. **1.** and **3.** are decorated with pinking and stitching and **2.** with pearls. Shoe 'roses' were made of silk, often edged with pearls and metal lace; heels low.

Heavy leather hunting glove; the gauntlet embroidered with silks and metal thread; silk lining and metal ball and tassel. *Left*: riding or hunting boot of buff leather, turned down to reveal a red velvet and gold braid-lined top.

Large hats (also worn at meals) were trimmed with feathers, cord or jewelled hat-bands or even with gold lace (**9**). **5.** and **6.** Conservative and older men wore small, simple ruffs or compound ruffs with flattened figure-of-eight sets. **7.** and **8.** A new standing-band was a semi-circular collar supported on a wired frame called a supportasse. The band was starched and plain; lace-edged or made entirely of lace. It was tied in front with cord band-strings with tassels. **4.** and **9.** The standing band is worn without the support – a development of the falling-band worn earlier in the century.

1600–1610

The farthingale was tipped up at the back and was much smaller by the end of the decade. Tight sleeves terminated in deep lace cuffs or hand-falls. *Décolletage* low and round; the whole figure overburdened with bows, sashes, lace and jewellery. Small-patterned fabrics were general.

1. Mary Queen of Scots hood with huge jewel; lace fan-shaped standing-band. Gauze and lace version on *full-length*.
2. Padded hair stuck with pendants; fashionable 'shaving-brush' feather.
3. Pinnacled hair with silk bows and jewel. 4. Stiffened halo bonnet of velvet, braid and pearls, edged with a row of small feathers.

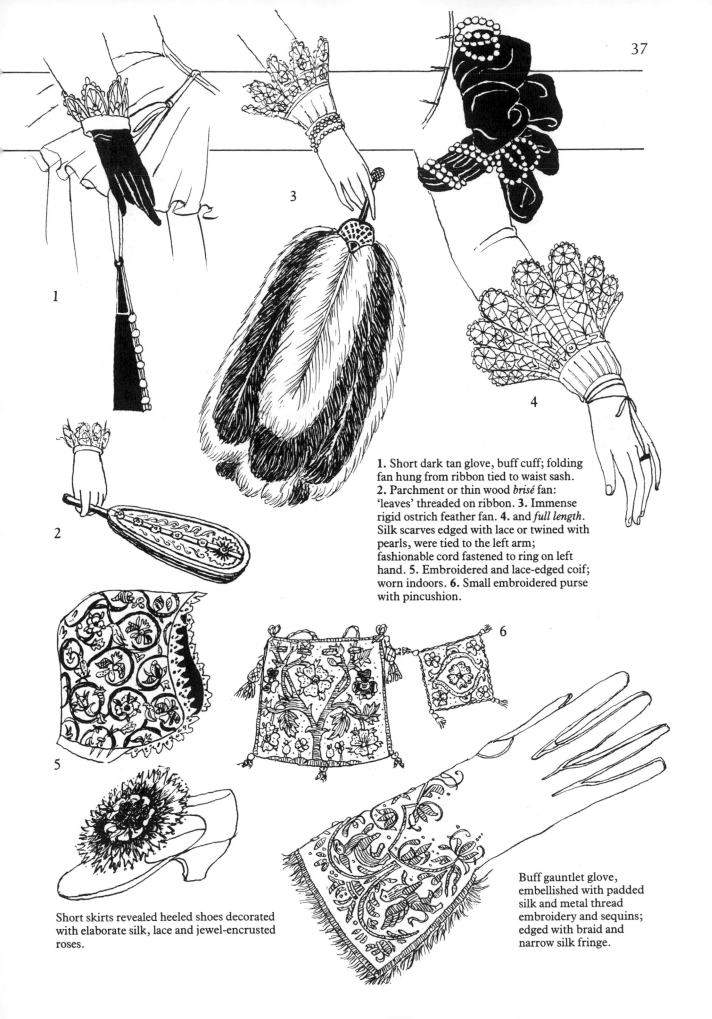

1. Short dark tan glove, buff cuff; folding fan hung from ribbon tied to waist sash.
2. Parchment or thin wood *brisé* fan: 'leaves' threaded on ribbon. 3. Immense rigid ostrich feather fan. 4. and *full length*. Silk scarves edged with lace or twined with pearls, were tied to the left arm; fashionable cord fastened to ring on left hand. 5. Embroidered and lace-edged coif; worn indoors. 6. Small embroidered purse with pincushion.

Short skirts revealed heeled shoes decorated with elaborate silk, lace and jewel-encrusted roses.

Buff gauntlet glove, embellished with padded silk and metal thread embroidery and sequins; edged with braid and narrow silk fringe.

1610–1620

Jacobean excess: over-patterned and still bulky. Tight doublet with deep cuffs; very full, long breeches; huge lace-edged standing-band; lace-edged silk garters and immense shoe roses; fur-lined and braid-edged cloak draped over shoulder; be-feathered hat so absurdly tall that, in portraits it is always shown on a table. Note fashionable cord earring.

1. By the end of the decade shoes were still painted but the roses were smaller: ribbon bows edged with pearls; embroidered clocks out of fashion. 2. White leather painted shoe with curved heel; huge rose; an embroidered clock which appeared on *both* sides of a blue silk stocking. 3. Buff gauntlet glove – the embroidery matches that of the doublet in the *full-length* figure. Note silk 'ruff' at wrist.

Moderately tall hat with braid and jewelled band and small plume. Lace standing-band; one pearl earring was worn.

When the French farthingale was discarded, a softer look was introduced: full skirts, natural waistline, narrow wings, loose sleeves with, often, huge hanging sleeves. The *décolletage*, as here, often so low and wide as to expose the breasts. An alternative dress fitted up to the throat. Skirts were usually short enough to show the shoes.

The decade saw the advent of a new head-dress: the shadow or cornet – a simplified version of the Mary Queen of Scots hood. **1.** Lace shadow under a stiffened gauze hood; lace standing-band. Lace was needle-point, reticella or cut-work. **2.** Small French hood with lace standing-band; ribbon tie. **3.** Lace-edged linen shadow with standing falling-band ruff. **4.** Elaborate lace shadow; layered standing falling ruff in figure-of-eight folds. Wrist-ruffs matched.

1620–1630

Everything began to collapse: high-waisted doublets had long skirts; sleeves were easier fitting; full breeches shorter and finished with ribbons; the old, stiff standing-band became the falling-ruff; cloaks crumpled; boots were crushed down.

1. White satin shoe with matching rose and slightly 'waisted' heel worn with black leather pantofle.
2. Soft, buff leather boot with contrasting scalloped turned-down top and deep, lace-edged boot-hose. Boots were becoming more fashionable for general wear as well as for riding and hunting.

Wide-brimmed felt hats were almost invariably turned up at one side and often ornamented with a long ostrich feather; jewelled hat-band. Lace-edged falling-ruff. By the end of the decade falling-bands were deeper and trimmed with bobbin, or rose-point, lace.

Women's clothes became even softer: high-waisted with full, smooth skirts, balloon – called 'virago' – sleeves. There was much lace, braid and ribbons. Jewellery was simple and hair frizzed or gently curled. Long skirts hid the shoes.

1. Fan-shaped standing-ruff; *décolletage* filled-in with lawn, and lace 'strips'; pendant and looped necklace. **2.** Spikey lawn ruff in tiers – a French fashion – with large pendant and wide chain. **3.** Three layers of starched lawn and lace collars, covered to the throat with ruched lawn. **4.** Large oval ruff, worn only by older, married women: note general mode of wearing long necklace. **5.** Buff glove with embroidered and lace-edged tabbed cuff.

1630–1640

The 'cavalier' look – common to England, France and Holland, was getting into its stride. Close-fitting doublets, slashed at breast and upper sleeve; sharply-curved high waistlines, accented by ribbons, with deep, over-lapping tassets; 'cloak-bag' breeches narrowing to the knee where they disappear into cup-topped boots with 'butterfly' spur-leathers; long hair; wide, lace-edged collars; gauntleted gloves and sweeping hats.

1

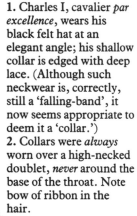

2

1. Charles I, cavalier *par excellence*, wears his black felt hat at an elegant angle; his shallow collar is edged with deep lace. (Although such neckwear is, correctly, still a 'falling-band', it now seems appropriate to deem it a 'collar.')
2. Collars were *always* worn over a high-necked doublet, *never* around the base of the throat. Note bow of ribbon in the hair.

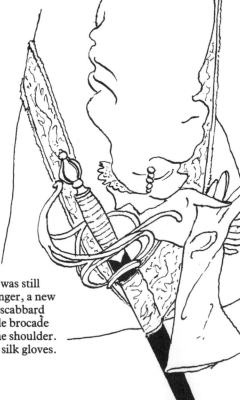

Although the sword was still carried in the old hanger, a new mode appeared: the scabbard thrust through a wide brocade baldric slung over the shoulder. Plain buff leather or silk gloves.

The cavalier lady favoured white, black, greys, greens, blues and pinks. The dress with its basqued bodice and stomacher; full elbow-length sleeves, with ruched or deep lace cuffs; deep lace collars or neckerchieves. Frizzed and curled hair; damp curls on forehead. Mannish, plumed hats emphasized an overall femininity.

1. Turned-up hat-brim decorated with artificial flowers, leaves, ribbons and a pendant; high-fitting, lace-edged, falling-band. 2. Lace-edged *décolletage* and matching cuffs; pearls in the hair, at ears and around neck. 3. Lace-edged coif, worn indoors well into the '50s. 4. Severe Puritan-style hat with lace-edged collar – worn by upper-class Protestant.

1640–1650

Silk, satin, lace and ribbons, soft colours and black and white: an age – if Van Dyke is to be believed – of great elegance. Doublets were loose and slightly high-waisted; sleeves slashed from shoulder to wrist; white shirts were flowing; the lace-edged collar was at its widest; bucket-top boots at their most extreme and lace boot-hose at its richest. Cloaks were short or great swathes of silk; silk sashes were worn baldrick-wise.

After cobweb-like reticella, needle-point and cutwork, rose-point, lace was worn almost universally. A thick, clotted lace, it enriched many garments and accessories.
1. and *full-length*. Collar stretched from the throat to over the shoulder. 2. Small collars were often caught at the throat. 3. Altenatively they were tied with a silk ribbon. Small collars were easier to wear with armour – a reminder that this was the time of the Civil War in England.

2

3

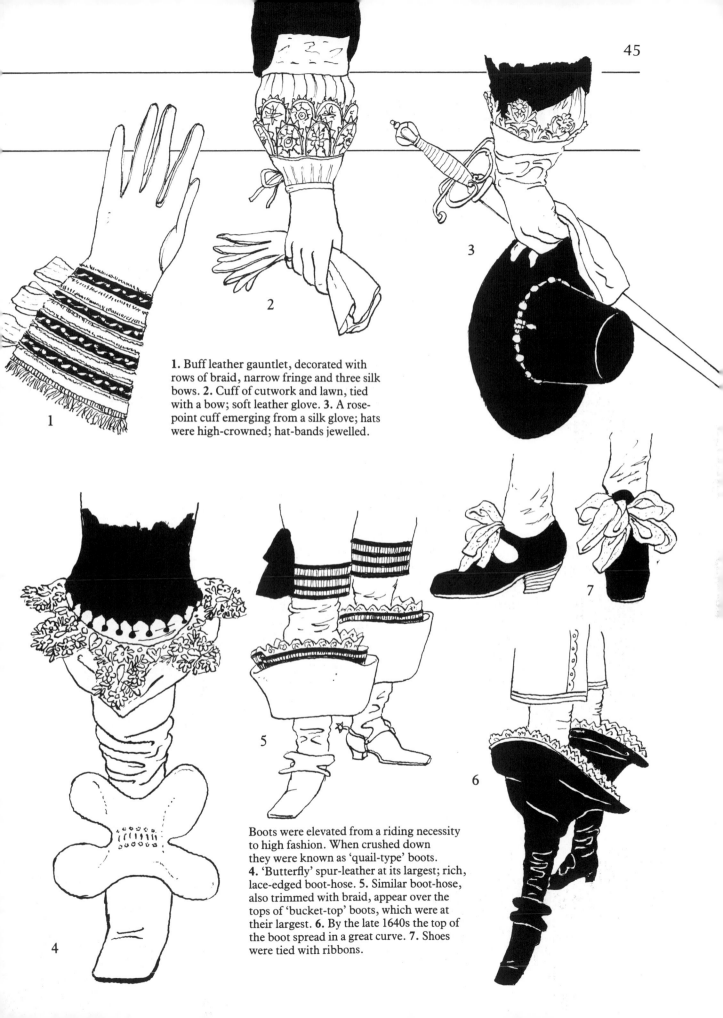

1. Buff leather gauntlet, decorated with rows of braid, narrow fringe and three silk bows. 2. Cuff of cutwork and lawn, tied with a bow; soft leather glove. 3. A rose-point cuff emerging from a silk glove; hats were high-crowned; hat-bands jewelled.

Boots were elevated from a riding necessity to high fashion. When crushed down they were known as 'quail-type' boots. 4. 'Butterfly' spur-leather at its largest; rich, lace-edged boot-hose. 5. Similar boot-hose, also trimmed with braid, appear over the tops of 'bucket-top' boots, which were at their largest. 6. By the late 1640s the top of the boot spread in a great curve. 7. Shoes were tied with ribbons.

1640–1650

For women, too, all was soft: silks and satins, lace and unstarched lawn, gentle velvets and furs, ribbons, dove colours, white and black. At the beginning of the decade, the waist was high, the bodice basqued with a deep stomacher. *Facing page*. By the middle of the decade, though, the waist was natural, an overskirt revealed an under, and sleeves were often paned; collars and cuffs deep and shoulders neckerchief-covered.

The shoe rose was still fashionable, mannish ribbons rare; heels higher.

An important new accessory made its appearance: the hood or chaperone. **1.** and **3.** Stiffened into a gable. **1.**, **2.**, **3.** and *full-length*. Neckerchieves were frequently worn, pinned at the throat. Silk scarves and fur stoles were also fashionable, as were muffs. Half-face, 'loo' masks were worn out-of-doors – a full mask was held in place by a button between the teeth.

Although short gloves were worn, long white, elbow-length gloves were more in fashion. Folding fans were in general use but there was a last flutter of a small rigid black ostrich feather fan, hung on a ribbon. White, lace-edged aprons were worn, even at Court.

1

1. Black gauze veil, covering head and shoulders; deep lawn, lace-edged collar. 2. Jewellery was restrained; confined to a single row of pearls, pearl earrings and brooches on bodice and sleeves. Note minute pearl 'cap', and small fur stole – the old 'flea-fur'.

2

1640–1650

In general, the prosperous middle-class wore garments which were more bulky than was strictly fashionable and with less lace and ornamentation. Men's cloaks were sleeved; their boots heavy; women were more likely to be 'in-the-mode', but favoured coifs under hats.

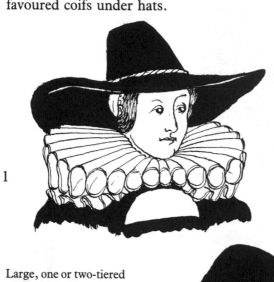

1

Large, one or two-tiered oval, 'old-fashioned', figure-of-eight ruffs were worn by older married women, especially in the country. **2.** Note that the simple hat is tied under the chin; lace-edged lawn neckerchief. **3.** Elaborate three-tiered collar, accented by a cluster of ribbons.

2

3

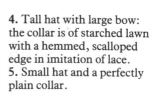

4

4. Tall hat with large bow: the collar is of starched lawn with a hemmed, scalloped edge in imitation of lace.
5. Small hat and a perfectly plain collar.

5

1650–1660

It is wrong to assume that everyone during the Commonwealth in England dressed as Puritans. Although more restrained than on the Continent, the upper-classes dressed richly: men in skimpy doublets, be-ribboned breeches and waist; women in low-shouldered dresses and pearls.

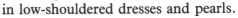

1. and *full-length.* The wide collar was replaced by a falling-band in the shape of a bib, with large bobble-ended strings. A black ribbon bow at the wrist indicated mourning. **2.** Indoor cap and knotted necktie. **3.** Boot-hose (without boots), worn over stockings and under shoes.

Below. Deep collar in heavy lace characteristic of this period. Pearl hair ornament and jewelled brooch.

Above. White silk chaperone with fur stole and ubiquitous pearl necklace.

1645–1660

Puritan/American

The Protestant and Non-conformist creeds, dubbed Puritan, became dominant in England in the 1640s and predominant during the Commonwealth of the 1650s. Its ideals were expressed in sobriety of dress and lack of colour. It was this style which the Mayflower Pilgrims took with them to America.

To a large extent, that which we dub British and American 'Puritan' dress was also worn by the Dutch bourgeoisie. **1.** The high-crowned wide-brimmed 'sugarloaf' hat – its only decoration a single hat-band cord. **2.** and **3.** Variations included the narrow-brimmed hat, and the black skull-cap, worn indoors and by scholars and clerics. **4.** Large or small plain white linen or lawn collar and cuffs. **5.** Heavy leather 'Cromwellian' boots had heels pegged with wood.

Puritan women's dress closely echoed that of middle-class fashion in cut; it even included laced stomachers. However, linen was plain and aprons functional rather than decorative. There was a marked absence of ribbons and jewellery. Long gloves were worn, although more for warmth than for show.

Although they would not have admitted it, the use of stark black and white was often beautifully dramatic. **1.** Black chaperone over a white inner hood. **2.** Huge sugarloaf hat worn with a tight hood and deep cape. **3.** Transparent lawn neckerchief pinned over a linen collar.

1660–1670

These clothes were high fashion in Europe in the late 1650s but did not become so in England until Charles II's Restoration in 1660.

Such dress was over-decorated and rather absurd: brief doublets with short sleeves revealed billowing shirts; 'petticoat' breeches terminated in frilled knee canons. Ribbons proliferated: on cuffs, at the waistline and, called 'fancies', on the petticoat. Lace trimmed every edge from cloak to bib. Periwig and peruke began their long reign. *Facing page*. In about 1665 in England, the vest or waistcoat, with tunic or coat, superceded the former style.

Black hats were heavily laden with coloured ostrich feathers.

The bib, *always* falling from the high collar of the doublet was almost universal. Some bibs were of plain lawn or linen and others were made entirely of heavy lace, or linen with borders of varying depth. This border was either pleated at the side or made in a curved shape. With very deep bibs the bobble-tasselled band-strings were often hidden.

Shoes were square-toed with fairly high heels, the tongue crossed by bows of similar or contrasting colour.

The sword was hung on a hanger which was simpler, yet heavier, than that fashionable at the beginning of the century. Here, the leather belt is hidden by a waist-sash. Canes were very fashionable.

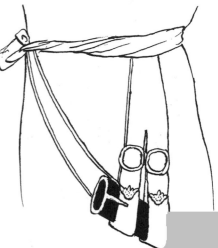

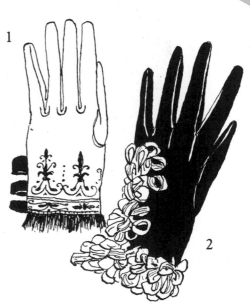

The majority of gloves were short and highly decorated. **1.** Buff leather with silver embroidery. **2.** Dark tan with loops of coloured ribbon.

1660–1670

Even on the Continent in the late 1650s women's clothes were neither as flamboyant or over-decorated as the men's, and the 1660s saw little change in the basic shape. However, the bodice was longer, and sleeves fuller; chemise sleeves fuller still and lace collars even deeper. Bows began to put in an appearance. Hair was frizzed and ringlets smart. Because it was fashionable at the English Court to be theatrically *déshabillé*, reference for day clothes are quite difficult to find for this decade.

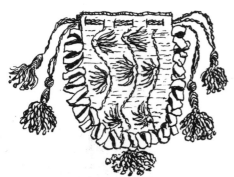

Small bag decorated with applied ribbon flowers. It is edged with loops of ribbon and heavy silk cord tassels.

1

2

The chaperone was still the favoured headwear.
1. Black silk chaperone covered by a fine black net hood; worn with a shoulder-covering collar.
2. Softly swathed lace chaperone, decked with bows, worn with low *décolletage*. **3.** Superb black velvet, white linen and lace-edged chaperone over a muslin hood; deep collar to match; as would cuffs.

4. Collar of raised Venetian needle lace: as with men's accessories many kinds of heavy lace were used.

By the 1660s little jewellery was worn, although a single string of pearls and earrings were a must. **5.** Chain and brooch with diadem-like hair ornament; softened by bows. **6.** Courtly looped satin sashes caught by pearls and brooches. **7.** Hairstyles accented by pearls.

Shoes were very high-heeled with long, narrow, slightly square toes. **8.** Cloth, buttoned over instep, with brocade clog. **9.** Leather with ribbon tie and bows on toe. 'Louis' heels.

1670–1710

From the reign of Louis IV, the 'Sun King' – 1643–1715 – France dominated the sartorial, as well as the cultural, world. It is safe to say that whatever was worn in France was worn in England, if less exaggerated.

However, the latter years of the century saw little dramatic change in fashion; narrow coats merely became wider and fuller at the hips; cuffs larger and the waistcoat more important. Hats grew larger and wigs curlier.

Basically the same accessories were worn throughout the period.

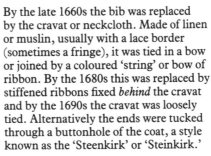

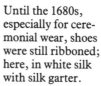

Until the 1680s, especially for ceremonial wear, shoes were still ribboned; here, in white silk with silk garter.

By the late 1660s the bib was replaced by the cravat or neckcloth. Made of linen or muslin, usually with a lace border (sometimes a fringe), it was tied in a bow or joined by a coloured 'string' or bow of ribbon. By the 1680s this was replaced by stiffened ribbons fixed *behind* the cravat and by the 1690s the cravat was loosely tied. Alternatively the ends were tucked through a buttonhole of the coat, a style known as the 'Steenkirk' or 'Steinkirk.'

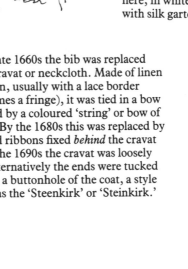

Swords were carried on wide brocade and fringed, or velvet and braid-edged baldricks. **1.** Method from the back. **2.** Front view, buckled.

3. Huge hats marked the era; adorned with great ostrich feathers, lace or braid-edged brims turned up in all manner of ways. **4.** and *full-length*. Huge muffs, plain or be-ribboned, were hung on sashes from the waist. **5.** Black leather, square-toed shoes. The tops were turned down to show the lining and the heels were almost always red.

6. The smartest gloves were gauntlets with deep fringes or bunches of ribbon. Short gloves had thickly embroidered and braided cuffs.

1670–1690

As usual, in the middle-class, men tended to dress more soberly than their womenfolk, with only a hint of decoration. Women, however, copied the latest fashions as best they could – if with less costly materials.

Men tied their plain or lace-bordered cravats with a ribbon, or merely twisted a plain neckcloth into a knot.

An alternative to the more general ribbon-tied shoe – one with a flat rosette bow.

Men's hats were decorated with ribbons or the turned-up brims with an edging of braid. Women wore versions of the chaperone – tied or untied – for country-wear, topped by wide-brimmed, flat-crowned hats.

1670–1680

A certain stiffness and heaviness began to creep into women's dress; the skirt was usually split and held back at the side in bunches, divided in the front to reveal an underskirt. Alternative dresses were softer; the overskirt often piled up into a kind of bustle. All dresses were low-shouldered with short sleeves; bunched chemise sleeves.

1

The chaperone was still worn. **1.** Often in contrasting colours and worn over tightly curled hair brushed out at the sides.
2. Presaging the high head-dresses to come, a lace cornet or coif with long lappets, worn with a coarse net scarf.

2

Full-length. Although jewellery was still generally sparse, when worn it took the form of brooches. *Right.* A *parure* consisting of a pearl and gold hair brooch, 'chandelier' earrings and huge breast pendant. A more rare form of jewellery.

1680–1700

As with men's fashion, there was no great change during this era except that, by 1690 there was a greater use of heavy embroidery, fringe and jewels, especially on underskirts. The head-dress grew taller and more ornate and decorative aprons were a smart feature. New accessories, such as the parasol, were introduced; face patches very fashionable.

1. Leather with red braid decoration and patterned silk heel; stiffened blue and green silk clog. 2. Leather with fine grey braid in rows and silver brocade front panel.

Full-length. By the late 1680s, the cornet was higher in front and decked with ribbon. **3.** and **4.** From 1690 to about 1710 the fontange, was the chief head-dress. It consisted of frills of linen and lace, one above the other; supported on a wire frame called a commode and attached to a cap. Lace lappets hung down in front and the bows of ribbon were known as 'knots'. **5.** A cornet, or a shallow fontange, worn with contrasting scarves.

Decorative aprons, as opposed to practical ones, had been a minor fashion as early as the 16th century (page 17) and also in the early 17th, but by the 1680s were high fashion. They were either short and made of silk, gauze, linen etc, embroidered and edged with lace; or long. Muffs were popular, as were narrow wrist-muffs.

Parasols were either round and made of lace or were octagonal and made of silk and fringe – a popular new fashion.

Fans were large: made of painted silk, edged with lace; or of ivory, imported from the Far East.

Long gloves, essential with short sleeves, were of plain or heavily embroidered kid. A ribbon bow on the wrist (also worn without a glove) was very *á la mode*.

1710–1720

The coat was tight-fitting in the body but fuller and more flared at the sides; easy-fitting sleeves ending in deep cuffs. Long buttonholes from neck to hem are a feature of this decade. The three-cornered, or 'tricorn', hat was carried, as it could not be worn on the full-bottomed wig.

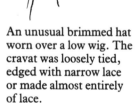

An unusual brimmed hat worn over a low wig. The cravat was loosely tied, edged with narrow lace or made almost entirely of lace.

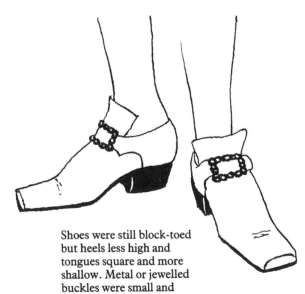

Shoes were still block-toed but heels less high and tongues square and more shallow. Metal or jewelled buckles were small and oblong.

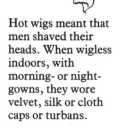

Hot wigs meant that men shaved their heads. When wigless indoors, with morning- or night-gowns, they wore velvet, silk or cloth caps or turbans.

Stiffness of silhouette, of materials and trimming were disappearing, to be replaced by a gentler, more feminine appearance. Except for Court wear, the train was shorter, and bunched-up skirts formed a bustle. Softer aprons were fashionable.

1. The fontange reached its maximum height in 1700, after which it gradually decreased until it was a standing frill.
2. In 1710 this was abandoned for the pinner, a circular cap edged on top with a double or single stiffened frill. Lappets were optional.
3. A small bag made from a netting technique called 'babila work'.

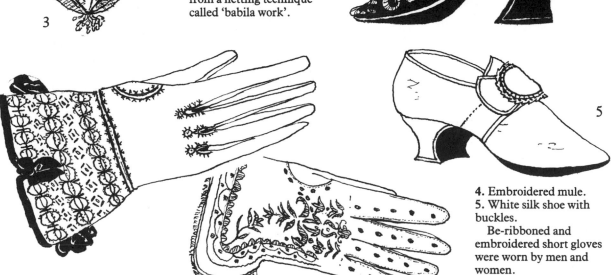

4. Embroidered mule.
5. White silk shoe with buckles.
   Be-ribboned and embroidered short gloves were worn by men and women.

1720–1730

Coats and waistcoats were even more flared at the hip; pockets at waist level; and edges trimmed with lace or embroidery. Stockings were rolled over the breeches and an English overcoat with deep cuffs – called a 'Redingote' in France – was very fashionable.

1. Cravat with tasselled ends. **2.** It was more fashionable to take the ends of the black silk wig-bow and tie them in a bow in front. **3.** and **4.** The equally fashionable black silk solitaire bow and band.

The three-cornered hat or tricorn, was fashionable until the 1790s. **3.** Small, trimmed with feathers and worn at a tilt. **4.** Smart beaux would sport a military-style, large cocked hat – the Kevenhüller – trimmed with lace or braid, with a loop, button, bow (seen here) or large cockade.

The dome-shaped, hoop petticoat appeared in 1710 but was not completely in vogue until the 1720s. The gown was often sack-, or sac, backed: full and pleated at the shoulders and made from soft or strong coloured silken brocades or satins.

Shoes, made of softly-coloured damask or brocade bound with braid had pointed, turned-up toes.

The pinner was almost universal and constructed in various ways, having in common a frill over the forehead; with or without lappets. **1.** The mob cap was only for 'undress' wear. It had a puffed crown and a lace-edged border which framed the face, with lappets known as 'kissing strings' or 'bridles'.

1

1720–1730

These two figures show French and English styles. The Frenchman (*right*), wears a full-skirted coat and embroidered waistcoat, and although a fashion-conscious Englishman (*facing page*) might wear the same, he was more likely to favour a narrow coat and no embroidery.

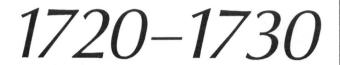

The tricorn (not so-called in the 18th-century) was *de rigueur*, worn over powdered natural hair or a neat wig.

1. A foppish man wears a diamond earring and a diamond and jewelled pin in his solitaire. **2.** Country-wear: large hat and lace-edged cravat. **3.** Folded linen or cambric stock – worn from 1735 – fastened by a gold and jewelled buckle.

Shoes were easy-fitting, fastened over the instep with small buckles made of silver, silver gilt, iron, cut-steel, brass or pewter; often set with stones.

Night and at-home wear caps. **1.** Crushed grey velvet with a tassel. **2.** Red velvet with a deep fur brim. Such caps were much favoured by artists and the intelligensia.

1

2

Snuff boxes were an obligatory accessory. Fops carried small fans on their wrists and favoured a walking stick, also hung on the wrist; huge wig or queue bows and immense fur muffs.

1730–1750

Clothes ranged from the formal Court wear: rich brocade embellished with silver embroidery and diamond bows, to the informal, *facing page*: satin gown with quilted petticoat worn over an oblong hoop. Transparent gauze aprons were plain or edged with narrow lace.

1. White silk with gold lace, edged with gold gimp. **2.** Rich brocade. **3.** and **4.** Shoes were protected outdoors with leather clogs, or pattens supported on iron rings.

6. A pinner, with a ribbon, was still worn but soon replaced by the round-eared cap or coif. **5.** and **8.** The coif was slightly bonnet-shaped with a frilled front border, often given a central ruffle or 'pinch'. It was made of lace-edged lawn, linen, gauze or net. **7.** Linen mob cap tied under the chin. **9.** A mob cap with a deep lace border, note the cross hung on a velvet ribbon.

Gloves were elbow-length – of plain or embroidered kid or silk, or knitted silk – *centre*. Mittens, with no fingers, were fashionable; made of embroidered kid, silk or cotton, or, like gloves, of knitted silk.

2

1. and *full-length*. Large straw hats, the French *bergère*, were very fashionable; the shallow or higher crown adorned with ribbon or flowers. **2.** A round-eared cap with a starched or wired frill: called a 'vast-winker'. Worn with a large-bead choker: **3.** A slouch hat worn over a 'vast-winker'. Lace-edged fichus were much worn, often stuck with flowers.

1

3

1750–1770

One must think of men dressed in bright brocades, silks and embroidered velvets following French fashion. The English were often more sober, military-style braid trimming being particularly popular. Swords were worn out-of-doors.

As horses were the Englishman's passion, riding boots were important footwear. They were made of black leather with tan leather tops and buckled over the knees of the breeches.

From c.1740 onwards, short, soft buff-coloured, gloves, with a short vent on the outside edge, became traditional.

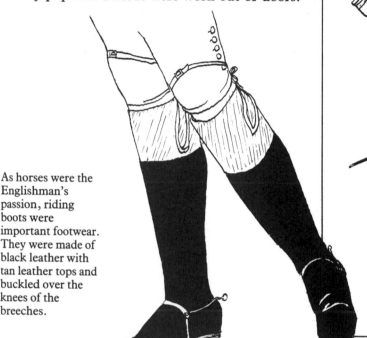

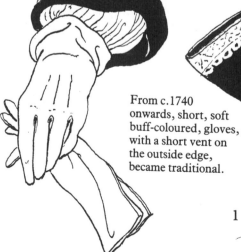

1. The tricorn, most lavishly trimmed with lace. *Full-length*. It could also be quite plain – the solitaire is very deep and full. 2. Country gentlemen wore white stocks tucked into the top of high-necked waistcoats.

1750–1760

Women's clothes were becoming more ornamented with ruched ribbon called 'robings' or 'fur-belows'; the petticoat trimmed with a gathered flounce. Short sleeves ended in up to three flounces, finished by lace ruffles. A fine lawn fichu might cover the deep *décolletage*.

Silk or brocade buckled shoe with high tongue; heels were about 4cm (1½in) high.

1. Pink and blue neck-ribbons match the gown. 2. Ribbon secures lace frills which match the sleeve ruffles. 3. Ruched ribbon tied with contrasting bow. Hair was decorated with ribbons, flowers and feathers. Small diamond or paste earrings. 4. Tilted straw *bergère* over a white linen cap tied with ribbon matching that on the hat.

1760–1770

The elaborately trimmed sack gown with a train – the stomacher was covered with bows called *échelles*. The sack was high-fashion until the end of the decade when it was worn only for formal and Court occasions. Lace tippets tucked into the bodice were fashionable.

Heels were high. **1.** Black leather with metal buckles. **2.** White satin with paste buckles.

3. *Bergère* hat worn over a net cap. **4.** and *full-length*. With hair dressed higher over pads, the 'Turkish' turban became fashionable. It consisted of a fringed silk or coarse net scarf twisted around the head and often finished by a bow. **5.** Bergère over a wired lace cap. Note that large earrings and chokers were worn with informal dress, in and out of doors.

1. The 18th century saw much exquisite diamond or paste jewellery in the form of bows – as here with a baroque pearl drop – birds or sprays of flowers **2.** Black silk bracelet pinned with an agate set in paste. Fans were at their most rich and ornate. **3.** Beautifully embroidered white silk shoe.

For formal and Court dress – that most influenced by French fashion – the oblong-hooped gown was obligatory; as was high-dressed, often powdered, hair, much jewellery, long white gloves and bunches of real or artificial flowers.

4. Black silk choker studded with brilliants; low net cap and enamelled aigrette. **5.** Wired lace cap set with brooches; diamond and pearl aigrette; similar brooches are pinned to the black velvet choker; diamond earrings. **6.** Starched lace and gauze cap edged with wired pearls; diamond aigrette; diamond girandole earrings; blue ribbon and pearl necklace.

1770–1780

In general, there was little change; coats cut rather more narrow. An interesting phenomenon of the late 1760s and 1770s were the fops or Macaronis – usually depicted in caricature. They dressed to excess: huge wigs; miniscule tricorns; tight-fitting, highly patterned garments; flowers and make-up.

Shoes with ultra-large 'artois' buckle. Pumps had large or small rosette buckles.

1. Macaronis – who paraded their effeminacy – wore large silk sword knots to indicate that the sword was for show rather than for use.
2. They also favoured extra long gilt or jewelled fobs for watch or seals, hung from the waist.
3. A new round hat, embellished by a ludicrously large button secured by cords. Such large nosegays were also worn by fashionable men who were not Macaronis.

All men carried canes but Macaronis decked theirs with bright tassels, often extra large.

English

High, Court and French-style fashion: superb gown of gold-spangled gauze, edged with gold ribbon and pinned with golden clusters. High-dressed hair topped by flowered and ruched lace. English informal and daytime wear was less ornate, usually worn without a hoop.

1

2

1. For most occasions, hair was increasingly powdered, given side curls and worn high. Consequently, all hats, such as the *bergère*, were tilted over the forehead. 2. Very high coiffure topped by yellow and white twisted silk scarves. 3. Pleated and ruched lawn and ribboned 'undress' cap. 4. Ribbons and lace. 5. A folding hood, or calash, worn from 1770 to 1790 to cover the coiffure in bad weather. It was made of silk mounted on cane arches. It could be pulled forward by the front cord.

3

5

4

1770–1780

French

Full Court dress was on the lines of that shown on page 75 but daytime clothes, among the aristocracy and at Marie Antoinette's glittering court, were no less exotic; often short-skirted, in rich fabrics, with much ribbon and lace.

1

2

Slipper-like pointed shoes of white or pale-coloured silk, had low 'Louis' heels.
1. Bound with narrow silk ribbon.
2. Decorated with a steel artois buckle set with beautiful cameos.

3

4

All the examples of headwear on these pages come from fashion journals which gave their bizarre creations fancy names.
3. Many were worn in England, a number even dubbed *Anglaise*, such as this hat or casque, adorned with huge imitation pearls. **4.** A bonnet *aux Bouillons*. **5.** A wired and lace concoction *á la paysanne*.

5

1. A magnificent gold and enamelled watch fob, worn by women as well as men.
2. Diamond bow and pendant necklace for formal wear.

3. A many layered mob cap *La Voluptueuse en coiffure de nuit*, worn to protect the hair. Formal coiffure – immense, tall, horsehair-stuffed wigs – could be a riot of fabrics, ribbons, flowers, feathers, beads, cords and tassels.
4. A fantasy named *Pouf á l'Asiatique*. **5.** A simple hat, *á la Henry IV*. **6.** An 'undress' creation called *á la bonne fèmme*. **7.** Two styles of parasol: small and fringed or large and plain. Coiffure decorated with only a bow and feathers.

1780–1790

Although French clothes in pre-Revolution days were still colourful, patterned and embroidered, English fashion was somberly restrained and elegant: the gentlemanly look. Wigs were worn less; hair more usually only powdered; various hats replaced the tricorn.

The stock had replaced the cravat; finished with a bow or a frill which was often decorated with a precious metal or diamond buckle.

Full-length. High-crowned buckled hat. **1.** Wide-brimmed hat with ribbon. **2.** Straw travelling hat. **3.** Bicorn with a cockade. **4.** A French bicorn with braid and a large button.

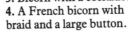

Shoes were now low-heeled; decorated with plain or ornate artois buckles. It was fashionable in France to wear English country clothes; including the elegant two-toned riding boot.

English

The 1780s in England were marked by the 'Gainsborough' look . It was also smart to wear this style in France. All was soft and simple: full skirts: whispy fichus and scarves; brushed out, grey-powdered hair and, above all, the 'picture' hat.

1

2

3

Most large hats were worn either at an acute angle or dead straight. *Full-length*. Black velvet trimmed with ribbon and ostrich feathers.
1. Country-style straw, with a lace 'curtain', tied under the chin with pink and red striped ribbon. **2.** Blue and grey silk decked with ribbons. **3.** Yellow straw with a 'roof' brim. **4.** Large mob cap, huge bow.
5. Black velvet trimmed with black and white striped, silk ribbon.

4

5

1780–1790

French

Before the Revolution of 1789, the *ancient régime* had its last fling with clothes which were rich, yet comparatively simple: 'bustled' skirts and fichued bosoms making women look like pouter-pigeons; large muffs and all kinds of outrageous headwear.

Daytime hats reached a size and degree of absurdity unequalled until those of the Edwardian era. *Full-length*. Black velvet with matching bows. **1.** Pink and black mannish hat decked with flowers. **2.** Roof-like brimmed hat – orange straw, green ribbon. **3.** Riot of blue and white striped cotton and silk worn over a mob cap. **4.** English-style pink straw, brown ribbon, worn over a veil.

1. A magnificent gilt and jewelled seal and chatelaine fob; it was smart to wear two. **2.** Diamond or paste spray brooch. **3.** Low-heeled silk shoe with small buckle. **4.** Small white embroidered bag with dark blue silk ribbon handle.

Hair was dressed less high but wider; for formal occasions crowned by head-dresses made of soft and starched fabrics, ribbons, feathers and flowers. These illustrations speak for themselves and were only a fraction of the possibilities open to fashionable women. Modified versions were worn in England. Note the 'chandelier' earrings.

1780–1800

American

Among the well-off, American fashion closely followed that of Europe throughout the 18th century – if, usually, less exaggerated. This is particularly true of the men, but women, by the end of the century, adopted some styles peculiar to America.

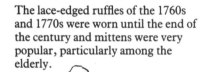

The lace-edged ruffles of the 1760s and 1770s were worn until the end of the century and mittens were very popular, particularly among the elderly.

The mob cap, in Europe primarily 'undress' wear, was, in America, more often worn for formal occasions. *Full-length*. With lace-edged frills.
1. A characteristically large and wide version with wide ribbons.
2. Perched on top of high-dressed hair.
3. High-crowned.
4. An extravagance to rival a Paris creation.

1790–1800

When the French Revolution swept away most excess in clothes, the English gentleman came into his own, with his well-cut, cut-away frock-coat; short, double-breasted waistcoat; skin-tight breeches; high stock and Hessian boots – or pumps for formal wear.

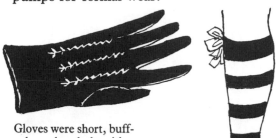

Gloves were short, buff-coloured or dark, with light stitching. Fops still dressed outrageously: striped stocking with ribbons at knee and slipper.

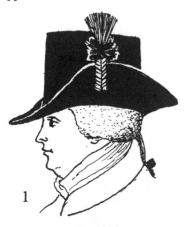

1

2

3

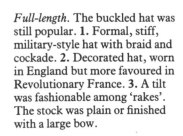

Full-length. The buckled hat was still popular. **1.** Formal, stiff, military-style hat with braid and cockade. **2.** Decorated hat, worn in England but more favoured in Revolutionary France. **3.** A tilt was fashionable among 'rakes'. The stock was plain or finished with a large bow.

1790–1795

Into the 1790s many women were still wearing dresses with natural waists, top-heavy with 'buffant' fichus and capes. Others adopted high-waisted gowns in soft materials; in England, in particular, retaining the swathed, pouter-pigeon silhouette. Hair was still long and curled, often powdered grey. Gloves worn day and evening.

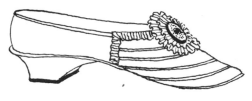

Silk shoe embellished with ribbing, braid and a jewel-studded rosette.

For the first time, handbags or reticules (also called ridicules and indispensibles) were essential with narrow skirts, and carried out-of-doors. Made of silk or velvet, they were often bucket-shaped and highly ornamented.

1

2

Headwear varied considerably. *Full-length, left.* A mannish hat with cockade. *Full-length, right.* A 'gipsy' straw, a very English fashion. **1.** A hat which bears signs of pre-Revolution frippery. **2.** Another typical English fashion – the large silk or muslin turban, always befeathered for day and evening. **3.** Large straw, liberally decked with blue ribbons. Bunches of flowers were fashionable for the bosom.

3

1790–1820

Court and Formal

As in many other periods, Court wear followed the old fashions. Until the accession of George IV in 1820, the hoop was *de rigueur*; the waist was high and materials softer, often, as here, draped asymmetrically, and decked with all manner of decorations.

Large feathered turbans reigned supreme. **1.** and **2.** Turban brooches in diamonds or paste and jet. **3.** and **4.** Court turbans, much entwined with grey-powdered curls. **5.** Fringed sash turban worn with formal dress: that is, elaborate day dress without a hoop. Low *décolletage* made necklaces important.

1795–1800

After about 1795, dress was dominated by an almost fanatical interest in everything Greek and Roman – the Empire or Regency look: thin fabrics, high waists, large silk or cashmere shawls and reticules. The hair was usually short but headwear as diverse as ever.

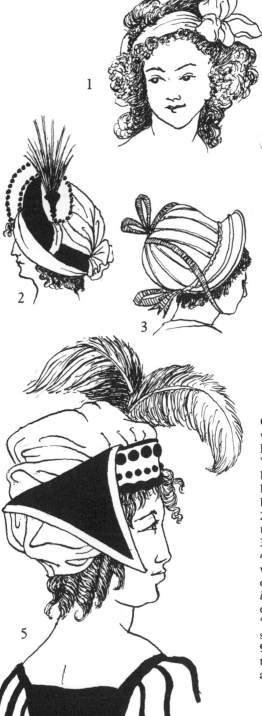

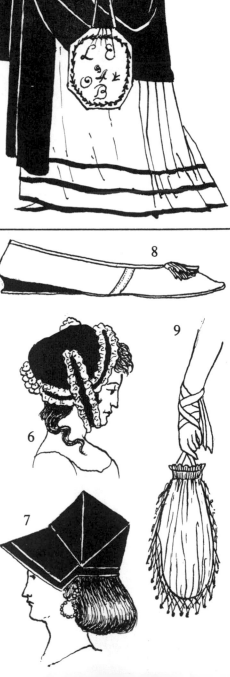

On the whole, headwear was small and head-hugging. *Full-length*. Very popular straw bonnet. **1.** Tousled hair, bound with a ribbon-bandeau *á la Greque*. **2.** Two-toned and beaded turban with aigrette. **3.** Ridged felt bonnet. **4.** Green silk scarf turban with tall aigrette, for evening wear. **5.** Turban *á la Greque*. **6.** Ribbon-edged cap. **7.** Severe 'helmet' hat. **8.** Very shallow slipper-shoe. **9.** Silk reticule; note the ribbon handles twisted around the wrist.

1800–1810

By the early 19th century, men's clothes were greatly influenced by George 'Beau' Brummel. Eschewing French silks and bright colours, he advocated cloth and dark shades; above all, plain, clean linen. The 'Regency Look' was exemplified by well-cut coats and breeches; curly hair.

Full-length. Hessian boots, were still fashionable as were top boots; dark leather with lighter turn-over tops; side loops for easier pulling-on. Gold fob seals were the height of fashion.

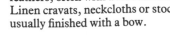

Top hats, of differing heights, had flat-topped crowns and brims which curved up at the sides. For Court and evening wear, the Opera, or 'cocked', hat, *left*, was of military origin: a soft crown concealed by two crescents edged with fringe or feathers; often with a ribbon cockade. Linen cravats, neckcloths or stocks were usually finished with a bow.

1800–1810

By 1800 the Regency or Empire look was well into its stride, although clinging Classical simplicity for day and evening was increasingly given non-Classical ornamentation. Long or short gloves; heavy, or cashmere shawls for day and flimsy scarves for night. Light and plain dress fabrics were off-set by darker accessories.

While dresses were simple, headwear, although on the small side, was extremely complicated and varied in shape; and made of all kinds of materials from straw to velvet, in white or bright colours and lavishly trimmed. **1.** and **2.** Capote bonnets with excessively deep, stiffened brims, blinkering the view. **3.** Straw bonnet softly draped and feathered. **4.** Stiffened velvet hat. **5.** 'Gipsy' hat with veil. **6.** Helmet-style hat. **7.** Severe bowler-style hat softened with bows. **8.** Poke bonnet, with ruched ribbon.

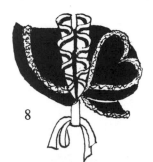

1. A square, 'box' reticule, covered in two-toned silk. **2.** Reticule of steel mesh trimmed with steel ribbing and pailettes; steel bead fringe. **3.** The 'sausage', or 'miser', purse; the centre opening closed by two steel rings. Made of netting, knitted silk and/or beads, it had been in use by men and women since the late 17th century but was more fashionable during the 19th.

Above. Rigid parchment fan for evening; elbow-length kid glove; short gloves of white kid printed with black designs and kid and green silk open-work evening slipper. *Left*. Three styles of silk and/or velvet evening turban head-dresses in which pearls or large white beads predominate. *Right*. Simple, open-topped 'bucket' head-dress, from which curls escape. Note spy-glass hung on a long silk ribbon.

1810–1820

The tail-coat continued to be worn, but an early form of frock-coat made its appearances, worn with tight pantaloons, often buttoned down the calf. Knee-breeches were reserved mainly for evening and Court wear.

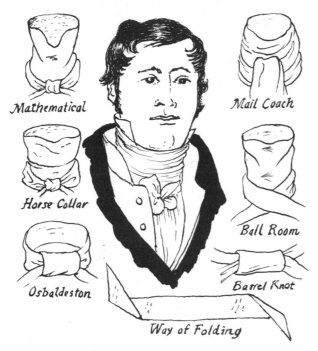

Mathematical

Mail Coach

Horse Collar

Ball Room

Osbaldeston

Barrel Knot

Way of Folding

With the shirt collar rising even higher, neckcloths became ever larger and were starched or supported on buckram or cardboard stiffeners. The cravat was tied in many scarf-like ways; given various sensible and non-sensical names.

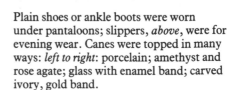

Plain shoes or ankle boots were worn under pantaloons; slippers, *above*, were for evening wear. Canes were topped in many ways: *left to right*: porcelain; amethyst and rose agate; glass with enamel band; carved ivory, gold band.

The majority of hats were tall, slightly narrowing towards the crown; brims shallow, with the exception of the example above.

'Humankind,' wrote T. S. Eliot, 'cannot bear very much reality' – and, in the realm of dress, women can, rarely, bear simplicity for very long. During this decade the line was still Classical but increasingly ornamented. Necklines were edged with ruff-like frills. Richly patterned cashmere shawls were still fashionable.

1., 2. and **3.** Although *capotes* were still worn, the poke bonnet was the most favoured style: high in the crown and deep in the brim, tying under the chin often with no bow. Velvets, silks or muslin were plain or ruched; trimming ubiquitous. **4.** A turban-like hat padded into a dome.

Reticules became more elaborate. *Full-length and adjacent.* Red velvet on a metal frame and embroidered cloth made to hook onto a belt. **5.** Blue watered-silk on an expanding steel frame. (Approx. 18cm (7in) diameter.) **6.** and **7.** Ankle boots were of kid, silk or cloth.

1810–1820

After the Napoleonic Wars had virtually ended in 1814, French fashioned revived. Bonnets predominated, and by the end of the decade were very high. *Full-length*. Pink straw and green felt. **2.** Straw, blue ribbon, black feather. **4.** Red and white silk. **5.** Green straw, yellow ribbons. **7.** White muslin. Other shapes: **1.** Purple and white plumed military-style hat. **3.** Blue silk, white feathered hat. **6.** 'Drum' in brown and white cloth, blue decorations.

Parasols in the 'Chinese' style were very popular. *Far right*. An unusual hinged variety.

1. A superb gold tiara set with ancient cameos in the prevailing Classic mode. **2.** Padded, jewelled turban decorated with imitation corn. **3.** Diamond or paste drop earring. **4.** Ballet-like slippers tied around the ankles.

Evening dresses were now not only much ornamented at the hem and given puff sleeves but more frequently coloured: often, strong shades with yellow a particular favourite. Many were quite short.

'Old-fashioned' mob caps were still worn indoors. **5.** After 1816 any indoor cap which tied under the chin was called a *cornette*. **6.** Pink evening hat with red and white plumes. **7.** Jewelled turban incorporating curls. **8.** Elaborate padded white silk evening hat decorated with flowers and yellow hanging, tasselled ribbons.

1820–1825

For men, tailcoats and frock-coats were still fashionable, but the nearly ankle-length greatcoat was an important new garment. Women's waistlines descended to natural level; sleeves were wider and fuller and skirts gored or pleated and heavily ornamented at the hem.

The top hat, or 'Topper', was cylindrical or curved out towards the top – the 'Wellington'. When breeches were worn with tails or morning-coats; cloth gaiters were often buttoned to the knees.

The hat practically supplanted the bonnet, was wide-brimmed and highly decorated, with ribbons and feathers. Neck ribbons were frequently left untied. Straw was a favourite material but lace was fashionable for festive occasions.

1

2

3

Muffs were huge and often made of fur to match the dress trim. Reticules were fairly large too. **1.** Felt, cloth or velvet heavily embroidered, on a chain handle. **2.** Heavy, two-toned silk. **3.** Gilt-tooled calf, covered with mother-of-pearl inlaid tortoiseshell. Slipper-like shoes were worn for day and evening but ankle boots were more usual, given flat, square toes in a contrasting colour.

1820–1825

Evening dresses were similar to those for the day except that they were always *decolletée* and often off the shoulders. Skirts were wider and excessively ornamented; trimming often taken up to the waist. Flimsy scarves were fashionable.

Evening slippers were usually tied with long strings wound several times around the ankle.

1

2

3

Full-length. Hats were worn for evening. **1.** Hair in an Apollo knot; pearl diadem and long *Glauvina* pins. **2.** and **3.** Elaborately decorated turbans for evening wear.

Long or short white kid gloves were plain, embroidered or printed. Jewellery was elaborate: earring, and choker – which was attached to ribbons.

1825–1836

Men's coats were fuller; shoulders wider to match the women's; no change of accessories. Women's sleeves were at their widest, achieved by stiff lining or pads: *Gigot* for day, or if closed with a cuff, called *Imbicile*.

1

Hats were huge; with high crowns and great turned-up brims; much bedecked with wide, stiffened ribbons, feathers, lace, flowers and leaves. The underside of the brim was usually equally festooned. **1.** A lace concoction, worn mainly in the summer or for festive occasions such as a fête or garden party.

1825–1836

Evening dresses extremely *decolletée*, the waist often pointed; the great sleeves, in 'Beret' form, single or double, were a great feature of this period. Dark, rich colours were as much favoured as light; skirts increasingly bouffant.

During this period, evening hairstyles were at their most elaborate ever – Apollo knots, curls and plaits. Styles were often achieved by false pieces. These *outré* creations were stuck with huge tortoiseshell combs of great beauty and imaginative complexity.

Full-length. Hair decked with ribbons and flowers. Great 'Persian' silk turbans were stuck with combs, jewels and plumes of osprey feathers. **1.** A befeathered, dark violet crêpe hat worn with a dinner dress.

1

1836–1840

During this period, men's clothes became increasingly shaped: tight-waisted and wide-shouldered. Except for riding and evening, the frock-coat was almost universal. Pantaloons were also beginning to be referred to as trousers.

Hats were tall and shiny with narrow, usually turned-up brims and given names. **1.** The 'Tilbury'. **2.** The 'Aylesbury'. **3.** The 'Turf' – very smart.

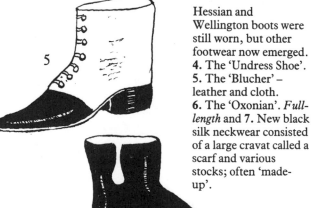

Hessian and Wellington boots were still worn, but other footwear now emerged. **4.** The 'Undress Shoe'. **5.** The 'Blucher' – leather and cloth. **6.** The 'Oxonian'. *Full-length* and **7.** New black silk neckwear consisted of a large cravat called a scarf and various stocks; often 'made-up'.

1836–1840

In 1836 the sleeve suddenly collapsed although it was still full below a dropped shoulder-line. The demure Victorian look, further emphasized by concealing bonnets and wider, fuller skirts, was coming in.

1. Cloth or leather elastic-sided boot.
2. Braided and beaded brown silk reticule.
3. Huge embroidered purple velvet muff.

4. The 'Bibi' bonnet, front and back view, showing the early shape where the crown and brim are at a compressed angle. Bonnet with horizontal crown and deeper brim, the back finished with a 'bavolet' – curtain.

1. and **2.** Two forms of the 'Babet' cap – be-ribboned and edged with frills. **3.** A revival of the 18th-century, 'round-eared' cap with wired brim and long, embroidered lappets.

With an increasingly large wealthy and idle middle-class, indoor and morning dress was becoming more and more important. Mittens or short gloves were always worn and, often, purely decorative aprons – and *always* a cap.

Straw or silk bonnets were decorated with ruchings, ribbons, flowers, leaves and even ears of corn. Flowers or ribbons often framed the forehead. For riding or hunting, women wore men's toppers with a flowing gauze scarf.

1836–1840

As with day dresses, evening and dinner gowns lost their wide sleeves, replaced by ruchings; *décolletage* was still very low; bodices tight and boned. Skirts were even fuller, trimmed and worn over many petticoats.

Evening headwear could still be elaborate. **1.** A silk turban. **2.** A plumed hat. **3.** A frilled cap. *Full-length* and **4.** Ribbons and flowers alone were more usual by the late 1830s, worn with ringlets.

Jewellery was fine and delicate made of filigree and pearls. Evening gloves were often finished at the cuffs with ribbons. **5.** A carved horn *brisé* fan.

1840–1850

The frock-coat dominated a gentleman's wardrobe; long-waisted, with short, full skirts, a deep collar and wide lapels – often edged with braid. Patterned or embroidered waistcoats; tight-fitting trousers which fastened under the instep.

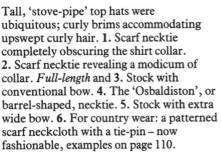

Tall, 'stove-pipe' top hats were ubiquitous; curly brims accommodating upswept curly hair. **1.** Scarf necktie completely obscuring the shirt collar. **2.** Scarf necktie revealing a modicum of collar. *Full-length* and **3.** Stock with conventional bow. **4.** The 'Osbaldiston', or barrel-shaped, necktie. **5.** Stock with extra wide bow. **6.** For country wear: a patterned scarf neckcloth with a tie-pin – now fashionable, examples on page 110.

1840–1850

All was droop: sloping shoulders; low-set, tight sleeves; only the horsehair lining to petticoats – the first crinoline – gave any sign of 'bounce'. Paisley shawls, swathed around the arms, emphasized the look of the helpless female and round-brimmed bonnets completed the picture of submissiveness.

1. Ermine muff: note the handkerchief. **2.** 'At home' bag: white satin, embroidered or painted. **3.** Green and white cloth tasselled outdoor bag.

The bonnet – crown and brim in a horizontal line – was worn almost everywhere, always tied so that the brim framed the face. Bavolets edged the back of the neck and trimming was moderate; flowers often on the inside edge of the brim. **4.** With a veil, which was often draped over the face.

Evening headwear
was minimal.
1. Feathers and
pearls – like the
later Stuart period.
2. Lace, ribbons and
flowers. **3.** A plain,
day-like bonnet with
ribbons untied.

Despite the emphasis on chasteness, evening dress
bodices were still cut provocatively low, revealing
the shoulders. The deep border, or 'bertha' re-
stricted movement. Arms were almost completely
bare; short gloves.

Only when riding or on the
hunting field could women look at
all aggressive. **4.** A curious mortar-
board-like riding hat. **5.** Man's
topper with a scarf; both women
wear mannish collars and ties.

An indoor cap of
frills of lace and
ribbons worn in the
garden. Parasols
were obligatory
outdoor accessories.

1850–1860

Style and cut were much the same, but garments proliferated. Apart from 'essential' morning, frock, dress and overcoats, a man could add one for riding, a Raglan cape and, seen here, a Paletot cloak with contrasting collar and slit armholes.

Although still sometimes referred to as a cravat, most neckwear was now deemed a tie; its most usual form a varying-sized bow or a 'shoe-string' tie.

The top hat was *de rigueur* for formal wear but a number of other styles came in. They included: **1.** Tweed cap for the country. **2.** A 'wide-awake' in felt or straw. **3.** A straw for the country. **4.** A rakish 'Bolinger'. **5.** Another straw for country or seaside.

In 1856 the weight of petticoats was relieved by the introduction of the 'cage' crinoline. Skirts were often in layer upon layer of flounces; materials sprigged, spotted, striped and plaid shoulders sloped demurely.

Some parasols were ridiculously tiny, but most were an average size decorated with ribbons and thick fringes.

The bonnet lost much of its deep crown and the brim, although framing the face in a circle, was set further back on the head. The bavolet was larger and often stiffened with buckram; ribbon ties were very wide and long. **1.** Muslin bonnet. **2.** Unpleated bavolet. **3.** Frill and flowers inside brim. **4.** Deep red silk.

1850–1860

The crinoline reached its widest: as much as 3.6 to 4.5m (12 to 15ft) in circumference, even for day wear. Large shawls were worn at any time of day; here – at home or in the garden – the fichu consists of ruched and padded silk.

The 19th century was the era for purses which were often made at home: a 'lady-like' accomplish-ment. *In the hand*: the 'miser' purse has a fringe at one end, a tassel at the other. The rest of the examples, of netting and beads, are all in proportion. Smallest, 60mm deep.

The 1850s saw a revival of the hat – favoured by the Empress Eugénie – worn in the country, by the sea (a 'Seaside' hat) or in the garden. It was not worn on Sundays and *never* in church. By 1856 it was called the 'Round Hat'. **1.** Straw, bows under the brim. **2.** Black straw with deep black lace curtain. **3.** Straw lined with pleated silk. **4.** White lace curtain and plumes. **5.** Straw 'lampshade' tied firmly under the chin.

Girls and women of all ages wore something on their heads indoors. **6.** When not wearing a hat in the garden then a similar concoction of lace and ribbons was worn. **7.** So many dresses had little collars that a brooch was a pretty accessory.

For evenings, any hair decoration – pearls only or with flowers – was set far back. Snake-like jewellery was fashionable; here, a brooch of blue enamelled silver.

1860–1870

The tailcoat was now worn only in the evening – a style which continues to this day in modern 'tail'. The morning-coat, in various forms was *de rigueur* for formal wear, and trousers were appreciably wider.

The top hat was still tall but much reduced after 1865.

Two types of boot: patent leather elastic-sided boot and two-toned leather boot with metal eyelet holes for lacing.

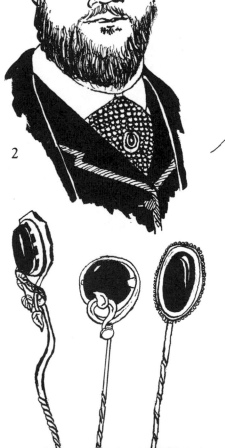

Very high collars and neckcloths were out. The only high versions were the 'Piccadilly' (**1.**), the first to be separate from the collar, as was the 'Dog', seen on page 124. Low collars included the 'Shakespere', **2.** and **3.**, and the 'Dux', **4.** Ties were wide and elaborately folded, **2.** and **4.**, or simply knotted, **3.** Tie-pins were a very important accessory, made of gold set with stones and pearls, in all manner of shapes.

Hats were increasingly informal; for leisure and sport. **1.** Straw with ribbon; the same shape made in felt. **2.** The 'Muffin' hat in ribbed silk and velvet. **3.** Domed straw cricket hat. **4.** An early form of the bowler.

For men, the 1860s saw the lounge suit as a more acceptable style, even if worn with stiff collar and tie. For women, the round crinoline lasted only until the early 1860s, after which it flattened at the front.

Two types of shoe available to women were severe patent leather boots and velvet boots studded with beads.

Hats were smaller and jaunty. **5.** The *Impératrice* made of felt. **6.** The *Casquette* of straw, feathers and huge bow.

1865–1870

In the early 19th century, some dresses were given a bustle effect by means of a pad worn behind at waist level but it was not until the late 1860s, when the crinoline disappeared, that a frame formed the first true bustle. On the left is a bunched up, short dress, revealing the feet. This period saw many materials used in one dress, excessive swathing and trimming.

Shoes were more fanciful. **1.** Black grosgrain, white and purple check and chenille pompom.
2. Black patent leather, red cords.

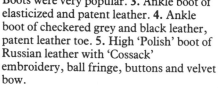

Boots were very popular. **3.** Ankle boot of elasticized and patent leather. **4.** Ankle boot of checkered grey and black leather, patent leather toe. **5.** High 'Polish' boot of Russian leather with 'Cossack' embroidery, ball fringe, buttons and velvet bow.

Evening accessories were rich and extravagant: necklaces (and matching earrings) of precious stones: ribboned and jewelled shoes; lace-trimmed fans and 'Greek' head-dresses trimmed with imitation ivy.

Evening dresses (by which one means those for balls, dinner and the theatre) were very low-cut with miniscule sleeves. Following day dresses, the skirt emphasis was to the back.

All hats worn with a forward tilt. **6.** *Impératrice* tied with a long scarf. **7.** Straw with lace ribbon streamers called 'follow-me-lads'. **8.** Old-style bonnets were still worn straight. **9.** Mannish cockaded hat worn when riding. **10.** Felt and ribbons; supported on curls.

7

8

9

10

1870-1880

By the 1870s, it was lamented that men were no longer so 'well-dressed'. Be that as it may, formally, the frock-coat held sway and the Norfolk jacket, 'suitable for any kind of outdoor exercise' was smart worn with knickerbockers and spats.

Collars were low or turn-over 'Shakesperes'. With coats buttoning high, the necktie was of less significance: a small bow perhaps. With yachting clothes, however, it could be as loose and full as one liked.

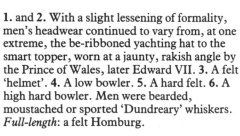

1. and 2. With a slight lessening of formality, men's headwear continued to vary from, at one extreme, the be-ribboned yachting hat to the smart topper, worn at a jaunty, rakish angle by the Prince of Wales, later Edward VII. 3. A felt 'helmet'. 4. A low bowler. 5. A hard felt. 6. A high hard bowler. Men were bearded, moustached or sported 'Dundreary' whiskers. *Full-length*: a felt Homburg.

1870–1875

When the crinoline was abandoned in the late 1860s, dress designers seemed reluctant to lose the full skirts. It would appear that skirts were, instead, simply swept up behind to create the first 19th-century bustle. At first it was rather bulky, the whole silhouette puffed out with ruchings, bow and ribbons.

The hair was curled and swept up to echo the bustle; consequently, hats had to perch at an acute angle. **1.** A nonsense of a hat: lilac frill, green ribbon and a wing. **2.** A yellow and black bowler with feathers and flowers.

3. A tiny orange bonnet smothered in flowers and tied under the chin.
4. The 'Dolly Varden' straw hat: the 19th-century's idea of the 18th. Parasols were edged with lace or much-pleated ribbon. *Full-length.* To our eyes, the parasol is held *upside-down*.

1875–1880

The bustle disappeared and the 'Cuirasse' bodice moulded the body, corset-like, from bust to hips, with a long, sweeping train. Skirts were elaborately draped and the trimmings excessively intricate. The use of different materials and trimmings in one dress and accessories was a feature of this period.

Outdoor bags were small.
1. A 'Chatelaine Pocket' of embroidered black velvet on a silver frame and chain which hooked on to a low belt. **2.** A similar 'pocket' echoing men's pouches of the 16th century. **3.** and **4.** Two calf-high leather, kid sealskin and fur boots. **5.** Black leather shoe with buckle and rosette edged with white kid.

6. Collar and jabot of lace and blue and white ribbons: such 'counterchange' was typical of this era. Ribboned yellow silk gloves embroidered and frilled.

1. White kid evening gloves were often ornamented: laced from wrist to elbow, ruched, beaded, and embroidered, sometimes from wrist to elbow. **2.** Pendants on a jewel-encrusted ribbon – also a daytime fashion. **3.** Embroidered silk, feather-tipped fan. **4.** White silk shoe with a buckle, ribbon and flowers. **5.** Pendant earrings, for day and evening, echoed long ringlets and deep trains.

Evening dresses followed the line of day dresses, with low, square *décolletage*. Sleeves were either very short or reached the elbow in a series of ruffles. Flowers and frills were the favourite form of trimming.

Bonnets differed from hats only in that they tied under the chin; both were made of felt, surah or straw and decorated with ribbons, lace, flowers, wings or birds. *Right*. A 'porkpie' felt hat. All headwear was pitched over the high-built hair.

1870–1890

The Wild West

The sartorial look of the Wild West is very familiar from countless 'Westerns' – tough cowboys and rustlers in wide hats and sturdy boots – tootin' their guns. Their clothes and accessories had to be strong, simple and hard-wearing. 'Civilians' wore modified versions of European styles and only the rough-and-ready homesteaders (*facing page*) wore anything like indigenous clothes.

Hats were made of good, soft felt. **1.** and **4.** The Stetson. **2.** The Planter's hat – light tan to white. **3.** The elegant Sombrero, trimmed with gold and silver, with its *Barbiquejo* or long cord chin strap. **4.** Tied neck scarf.

Other accessories included this 'Prarie' cartridge belt; beautifully silk embroidered leather holster and belt, and plain leather Mexican holster.

1. Homemade sunbonnet, starched, or stiffened with cardboard or light wooden inserts. 2. A black felt slouch hat. 3. A woollen hat. Leather gauntlet gloves were richly embroidered or sewn with beads and fringed.

Apart from his hat, the cowboy's most costly accessory were his boots, usually of calf-skin and always square-toed.
4. Two-toned extra high boot.
5. Embroidered with coloured thread.
6. Leather cut-out star. 7. Ankle boot. Spurs were fine examples of the blacksmith's art and craft and included:
8. California spur. 9. and 10. Texas spurs. They were fastened on by all kinds of leathers or by metal chains and hooks.

1880–1890

Left. Conventional men wore morning-coats but the 'Masher', 'Chappie' or 'Piccadilly Johnnie' favoured a suit or a refer. *Right.* For very informal wear, a lounge suit with a 'jockey vest' was worn.

1. Ankle boots were worn but a black patent shoe with an elastic gusset was smarter. **2.** Beige cloth spats were always fashionable.

3. Cricket cap which matches the suit. **4.** Tweed deerstalker for country and bicycling. **5.** The bowler was higher, for summer light coloured or checked. **6.** Straw tennis hat with deep band. **7.** Blue fabric seaside or yachting cap matching the jacket.

1880-1884

By the close of the 1870s, the bustle began to reappear but from about 1880 to 1883, the very tight, swathed 'hobble-skirt' was worn by the ultra smart. It was also worn concurrently with the reinstated bustle, which was usually puffed out and lacked the long train characterizing the whole of the previous decade. For winter, especially, colours were very dark; lighter for summer.

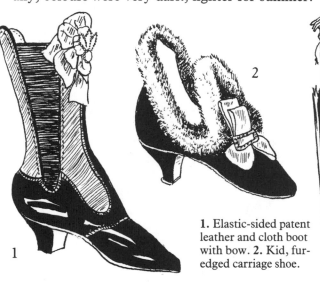

1. Elastic-sided patent leather and cloth boot with bow. **2.** Kid, fur-edged carriage shoe.

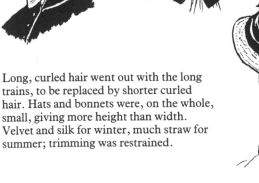

Long, curled hair went out with the long trains, to be replaced by shorter curled hair. Hats and bonnets were, on the whole, small, giving more height than width. Velvet and silk for winter, much straw for summer; trimming was restrained.

1884–1890

Until about 1888 this was the age of the huge bustle projecting like a shelf – 'whereon a good-sized tea-tray might be carried' – as disfiguring a style as the French farthingale and panniers. Skirts were swathed and looped in all manner of ways. Dark velvet, jet-edged jackets and capes were fashionable.

Full-length. Small muffs were fashionable. So too were umbrellas with fancy handles, cords, tassels and ribbons. Leather handbags were quite plain.

As the bustle extended, so hats became taller, perched on narrow, neat heads. Ribbons, whole birds, and feathers were the favourite form of trimming.

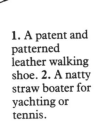

1. A patent and patterned leather walking shoe. 2. A natty straw boater for yachting or tennis.

1. A tasselled blue gros-grain evening bag. 2. A large (probably home-made) 'at home' bag of brown, gold-embroidered cloth, with a fringe.
3. Decorative aprons were often worn, made of silk, relatively plain or ribboned.

Morning wear was less ornate than for outdoors; lace scarves were popular. For the evening, dresses were deep-bustled with plunging necklines; little headwear.

4. Breakfast lace and ribbon cap; the lace scarf reached to just below the waist. 5. A popular painted paper 'Japanese' fan. 6. White watered-silk evening shoe, the toe studded with beads. The evening 'boot' is made of bronze kid with silk lacing; beaded rosette.
7. Tortoiseshell hair comb and hair-pin.

1890–1900

By this date the high standard of English tailoring was world-famous and formal wear remained the same until the Second World War. Informal clothes were increasingly 'countryfied' – even if often worn with stiff collar and tie.

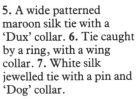

Full-length, left: The straw hat typifies this decade in that it was the only headwear which could be worn by all social classes.
1. The tweed flat cap was worn by gentlemen only for country wear. **2.** The 'Terai' – a bowler-like hat with a turned-up brim.
3. A hard felt bowler.
4. A tweed 'helmet', resembling a military pith helmet.

5. A wide patterned maroon silk tie with a 'Dux' collar. **6.** Tie caught by a ring, with a wing collar. **7.** White silk jewelled tie with a pin and 'Dog' collar.

1888–1893

In 1888 the huge bustle was replaced by padding until c.1890 when it disappeared for good, giving a smooth, narrow, slightly hip-emphasized silhouette. Slim sleeves were puffed at the shoulders; the waist dipped and the bust-line began to be emphasized.

With the emphasis on the bosom and high neck, separate 'collarettes' and jabots were very important – made of lace, net and ribbons.

1

2

1. Black leather boot with attached tweed spat. **2.** Patent leather and silk at-home shoe.

5

With hairstyles still close, hats and bonnets were small. **3.** and **4.** Stiffened ribbons give height. **5.** A felt mountaineering hat. **6.** The exception in size was the summer straw.

3

4

6

1893–1900

Restraint did not last for long and until 1897 the huge gigot or 'leg-of-mutton' sleeve reigned supreme. So too did wide revers – often contrasting with the dress – and skirts were full from the hips. Full jabots accentuated bosoms. *Facing page*. After 1897 sleeves were narrow and given an epaulette shape or small puffs, bosoms drooped.

With narrow waists and the fashion for wearing blouse and skirt, belts became all-important: made of tooled, beaded and silver-decorated leather or cloth.

Hats could be very wide and high – gorgeous in colour and exuberant in decoration – or very small. For summer, lace and straw were popular.

Hair was dressed more fully and for evening given a bow, often stuck with an ornate pin or a comb. Smart women wore Art Nouveau Jewellery, such as the illustrated diamond, sapphire and emerald peacock-feather brooch.

1. Patent leather boot with ribbon-embroidered upper.
2. Plain cloth or leather.
3. Snakeskin.
4. Patent leather at-home pump with contrasting pattern and bow.

By the late 1890s, hats were still small. 5. Summer straw. 6. A tipped-up toque with roses and a veil. 7. A summer boater. Hatpins, in an immense variety of materials and shapes, were ubiquitous.

1900–1910

The early years of the century saw little change in men's clothes – formality in frock coat (or, as here, a Chesterfield) and topper; informality in suit and boater. There were motoring overcoats, and the Norfolk jacket with plusfours were smart for the country.

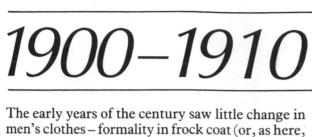

The variety of stiff colours was infinite: worn with the most casual of wear. Ties: narrow or soft bows.

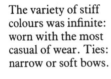

1. Although the fine straw Panama hat originated in the 1880s, by the 1900s it was deemed the hat 'par excellence'.
2. A Panama worn for tennis.
3. 'Swells' sported grey silk toppers.

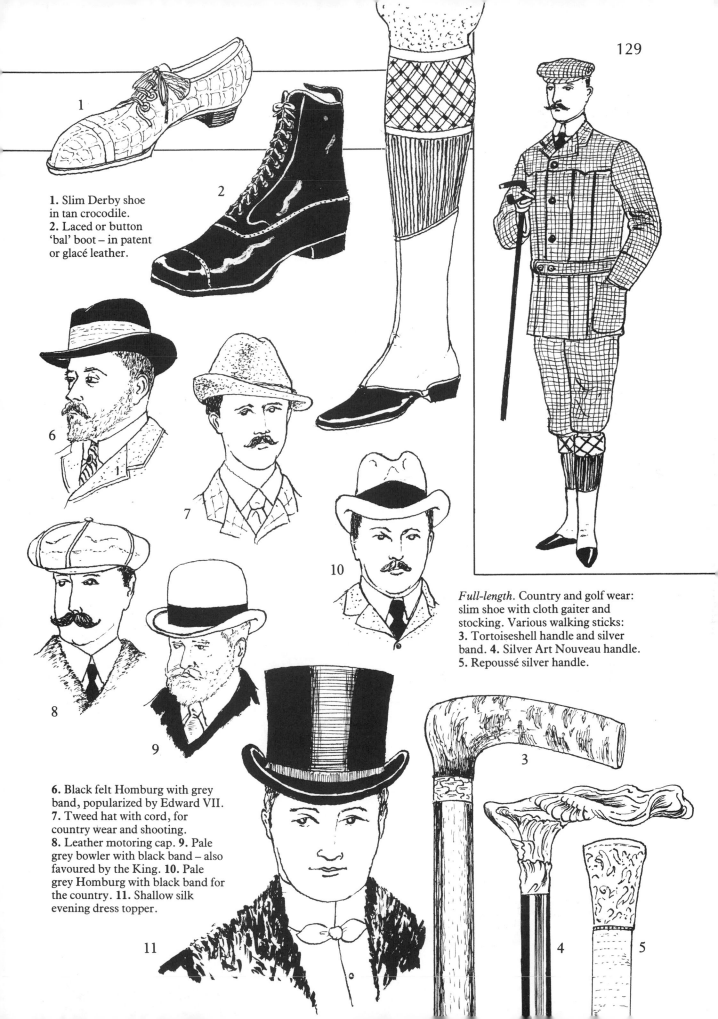

1. Slim Derby shoe
in tan crocodile.
2. Laced or button
'bal' boot – in patent
or glacé leather.

Full-length. Country and golf wear:
slim shoe with cloth gaiter and
stocking. Various walking sticks:
3. Tortoiseshell handle and silver
band. **4.** Silver Art Nouveau handle.
5. Repoussé silver handle.

6. Black felt Homburg with grey
band, popularized by Edward VII.
7. Tweed hat with cord, for
country wear and shooting.
8. Leather motoring cap. **9.** Pale
grey bowler with black band – also
favoured by the King. **10.** Pale
grey Homburg with black band for
the country. **11.** Shallow silk
evening dress topper.

1900–1908

The 'Edwardian summer' saw clothes either at their most feminine and frivolous: garden party frocks all lace, ribbons and soft colours or (*facing page*) at their most severe: tailor-mades in plain colours. The 'S'-bend or 'Gibson Girl' look was *the* fashionable, sought-after silhouette.

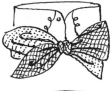

High separate collars were either mannish with bows, or froths of starched, embroidered linen or lawn; or of lace or broderie anglaise.

1. Pale leather with velvet bow and cuban heel. 2. Black patent house-shoe. 3. Many-strapped leather. 4. Patent or calf boots with cloth uppers were still very fashionable.

8

5. Fur muff decorated with tails. **6.** Fur tie, embellished with deep lace bow. **7.** Medium-sized cloth or velvet bag with metal chain. *Full-length*. It was smart to carry a small purse.

5

6

7

9

14

Hats became larger once more, balanced on piled and swept-up hair. **8.** Many-layered pleated straw brim with huge velvet bow. **9.** Black velvet, ruched ribbon and silk roses. **10.** Veiled bowler for riding. **11.** Leather motoring cap with chiffon scarf. **12.** Straw and ribbon for tennis or seaside. **13.** Shallow-crowned, wide-brimmed, with large silk bow. **14.** Jaunty summer straw decorated with silk roses.

10

11

12

13

1900-1908

The 'Gibson Girl' silhouette was no more evident than in evening dress where the low 'pouter' bosom was decked with lace, bows and jewellery. Shoulders were provocatively bare, sleeves short and trains immensely long. Fabrics: heavy silks, satins and soft nets.

1. Diamond corsage ornament strung from shoulder to shoulder. 2. Satin and silk shoe. 3. Horn Art Nouveau comb. 4. Pleated paper 'Souvenir' fan, with mirror. 5. Gauze fan embroidered with sequins and spangles.

6. Beaded silk bandeau. Huge hats were worn at the theatre or for dinner in smart restaurants. 7. Velvet-edged straw with osprey feathers. 8. Pink ruched silk, looking like the underside of a mushroom, and ostrich feather.

1908–1911

Smartly dressed men accompanied women who had abandoned the 'S' silhouette for a narrow, 'Grecian' or 'Russian' line: high-waisted long coats and often long-trained skirts. Costumes were softly draped or simply tailored: decoration spare. Fabrics: cloth, silk and ninon; colours clear and sharp; very few patterns.

A slight lessening of formality meant that men could wear brown bowlers even in town.

1

Narrow figures were topped by some of the largest hats in history: the 'My Fair Lady' headwear, making women look like heavy-headed flowers on thin stalks. **1.** Beaded and embroidered lilac silk turban. **2.** Ruched and crushed Prussian blue silk. **3.** Black velvet, yellow silk bow, white ostrich plumes. **4.** Dark green silk; pink and white roses.

2

3

4

1911–1915

Men could appear in town in dark lounge suits and homburgs, with women dressed in the new 'harem' ankle-restricting skirts which could also be hunched at the hips; coats long or short. The look was svelt, clean, sharp and assertive; women even sported canes.

The wing collar and small bow tie were ubiquitous. Patent leather shoes with cloth uppers or spats were equally general.

3

4

5

1. Patent leather boot with check cloth upper. **2.** Heavy metal buckle on velvet shoe.

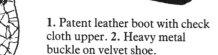

This was the era of the large bag – lampooned by *Punch*. **3.** Black leather on a very long chain handle. **4.** Brown leather 'briefcase' bag. **5.** Smaller crocodile bag with tassels and a cord handle. **6.** Beaded or embroidered bags were everywhere.

1

2

6

11

7

8

Turbans, in style
harking back to the
Regency, were worn
with full evening dress.
7. Red silk, edged with
beads, topped with an
aigrette and caught
with a brooch. **8.** and **9.**
Feathered hats worn
for restaurant dinners.
10. Black satin shoe
with jewelled silk rosette.

9

10

For evening, the waist was high, *décolletage* very
low; dresses often in two parts; tunic and skirt,
which was usually trained; made of silks and
diaphanous materials, embroidered and headed –
Greek-style flights of fancy. Fur-edged coats and
capes very fashionable.

13

14

12

11. One of the few still large hats:
stiffened black felt; worn with an
ostrich feather ruffle. **12.** A tulle
ruffle is worn with this brown hat,
given height by two feathers.
13. Ribboned black straw. **14.** Grey
silk toque. **15.** An extravaganza in
black velvet: a pillbox surmounted
by a stiffened spiral.

15

1915–1919

Fashion paid only a nod towards the Great War of 1914–1918, with some military-style clothes and simplicity. Change, however, occurred by way of shorter skirts and, as *Vogue* but it: smartness no longer lay 'in slim economy of line'. Bulk, at the hips, sometimes at the shoulders, was the norm.

Gloves were delicate. Beige suede with glass button and white kid, black silk embroidery.

With shorter skirts the still fashionable leather and cloth boot was even more in evidence. Heels were high for boots and shoes; shoes strapped or with buckles.

1. Dark blue satin and white cord bag. **2.** Black velvet with 'shaving-brush' aigrettes. **3.** Yellow velvet with silver lace veil; paradise feather.

Evening dresses echoed day-time bulk, often with a 'fish-tail' train. The velvet and beaded tulle example is typical of the semi-formal gowns which, with a hat, were fashionable for restaurant dinners.

Day-time hats were wide or comparatively small. **4.** Black satin with fluted hand and brim. **5.** Wide hats were often worn at a tilt: green velvet and jet. **6.** A tricorne toque of rose chenille braid, worn over one eye. **7.** Brown felt, gold braid – a military air. Great stoles and huge muffs were fashionable: here, in popular skunk.

8. Large feather fans were popular, 60cm wide: here, of peacock feathers. **9.** Heavily beaded bag for day or evening; a style which lasted into the 1920s. **10.** and **11.** For evening, a bead and feather bandeau and black tulle frills mounted on a jewelled comb.

1919–1930

After the horrors of the trenches, men turned with relief to peace – and to all kinds of new casual wear: blazers, pullovers, soft collars. The cry 'Anyone for tennis?' was heard and eccentric fashions were set by the young Prince of Wales, Noël Coward and Cecil Beaton.

1. Derby boot: glacé kid. 2. Black or tan calf. Oxford brogues in calf: 3. Light brown. 4. Blue and beige. 5. Light and dark brown calf.

6. Check tweed golf cap. 7. The bowler was still correct town wear. 8. Tropical white topee – sometimes worn in England. 9. and 10. Black and grey trilbys. Sophisticates sported long cigarette holders; the more conventional, pipes.

1919–1925

After the Great War, the emancipated 'flapper' was born but immediate post-war clothes were slow to reflect this change. Even so, the waist was lowered and the silhouette became tubular – skirts remained longish. Chinese paper parasols were all the rage and beige *the* colour.

Many early 1920s hats were wide-brimmed and worn low over the eyes. **1.** Beige felt, yellow ribbon. **2.** Pink straw, black crown and pink ribbon. **3.** A bandeau of twisted and bowed lilac silk.

The cloche appeared in about 1924. **4.** Blue straw, beige ribbon, worn with matching fashionably long scarf. **5.** Folded beige silk with black satin bow.

When Tutankhamun's tomb was discovered in 1922, it produced a flood of Egyptian-style clothes and accessories. **6.** Black silk and silver lace hat. **7.** White leather shoes – white stockings were general. **8.** Brown leather. Other shoes were T-strap: *full-length*.

1919–1925

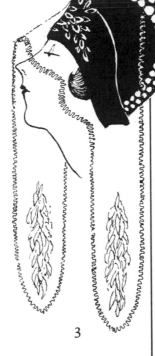

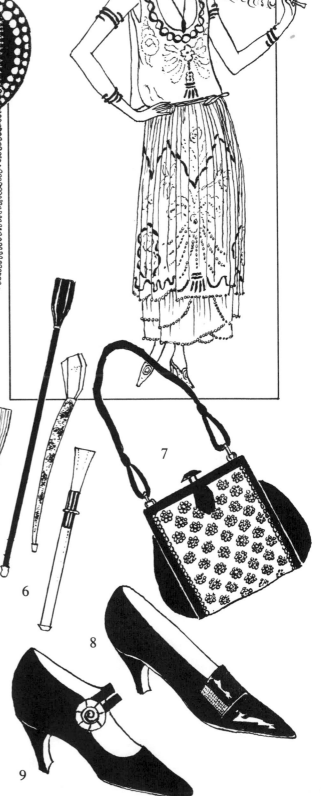

1. 'Egyptian' cap: blue velvet, gold braid; typical long earring. **2.** A cubist variation. **3.** Cap of stiffened black satin, silver leaves and pearls. Wired gauze embroidered veil.

Evening dresses were low-waisted and sleeveless; skirts in layers. This dress is made in *in crêpe de Chine*, embroidered with jet and brilliants.

4. 'Vanity' or make-up case of black enamel and diamonds. **5.** Batik-printed silk fan. **6.** Cigarette holders of ivory, horn, tortoiseshell, etc. **7.** Black and grey suede sewn with pearls. **8.** Black satin with white rosette. **9.** Black satin with cut steel buckle.

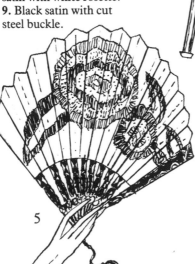

1925-1929

By 1925 the 'real' '20s look (chic was *the* word) was established – short skirts and hair, cloche hats, fox furs, vivid colours and jazzy patterns. For evening, simplicity ruled: a tube accentuated by a sash, uneven hemlines, bangles and very long necklaces.

1. Brown seal-skin and python-skin. 2. Brown brogue – emulating the men. 3. Black satin with diamond buckle: for dinner or party. 4. Brightly patterned silk for evening.

5. Black patent with snakeskin bands; zip fastening. 6. Silk – which could be beaded or embroidered: for day or evening.

For hats, the use of two colours was considered important. 7. Green and white felt. 8. Navy blue and beige in baku – a linen-like straw. 9. Black straw with green flowers. 10. Brown with old-rose. Chic shoulder bunch of artificial flowers.

1930–1939

For smart town-wear: the double-breasted pin-striped suit, trilby, gloves and calf shoes. For the country: tweed sport's jackets and caps; polo-necked sweaters; two-tone shoes. Trousers were wide, with turn-ups.

Old-fashioned men still wore toppers, city-gents' bowlers but the young and smart favoured dark or light trilbys worn at a jaunty angle; or tweed caps.

Ties in all kinds of patterns were fashionable as were scarves worn with blazers and jackets.

This was the age of two-tone brogues – often referred to as 'co-respondants'. Variations were endless. **1.** and **2.** Two possibilities. **3.** The new sandal for very casual wear. **4.** The 1934 slip-on.

1929–1935

By the end of the 1920s, skirts were long again; the silhouette narrow. 'Smart' replaced 'chic' in the fashion vocabulary; a certain hardness was evident. Sombre colours: navy blue, 'nigger' brown, black, grey. Much fur and fur trimming.

Hats were usually small, worn at an angle. **1.** The exception – a deep straw with navy crown. **2.** A ribboned brown beret. **3.** Black felt, gauze ribbons and brim. **4.** Straw and navy ribbon. **5.** Fashionable gloves were gauntlet-length: white and beige kid, stitched with black or 'cowboy' fringed.

1

5

2

4

3

Jaunty little head-hugging hats were worn over one eye. Striped rayon – white, blue and beige – matching the extravagantly-tied scarf. Very 'smart' two-toned calf court shoe were also worn.

1929–1935

Handbags were usually flat envelopes or *pochettes*. **1.** Black patent with 'gold' clasp. **2.** Navy and white in a typical Art Deco design. **3.** Navy patent court.

Full-length. Wide, shallow hat in Duchess of Kent-style. **4.** Grey felt with navy and red feather. **5.** Green grosgrain knotted turban with matching scarf. **6.** Wine-red felt. Long gloves for day.

Full-length, right. Typical backless evening dress. Worn with it: **7.** Diamond, onyx and pearl pendant. **8.** Red leather sandal. **9.** Diamond clip. A pair of such clips was worn each side of the *décolletage*.

1935–1939

War loomed again and a general cynical *insouciance* and defiance were echoed in women's dress. By 1938 skirts were shorter and shoulders wider, decoration very spare, colours generally dark. Fox furs were still very smart.

Hair was coiled at the nape and swept up; hats perched. **1.** Tiny tipped silver fox hat with matching small muff. **2.** Black felt with a touch of ribbon. **3.** Impudent straw with navy quills. **4.** Black straw with yellow cord snood.

5. Beach clog in grey tweed with hinged wood sole. **6.** 'Peeptoe' black suede sandal with wedge heel. **7.** Blunt-toed black patent court.

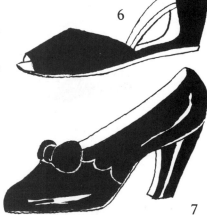

1939–1947

The Second World War had a marked influence on fashion. Not only were women serving in the Forces and involved in all kinds of War work but clothes rationing made any excess (except for hats) impossible. The wrap-over, tie-belted, square-shouldered coat, was typical of the no-nonsense masculine-style look.

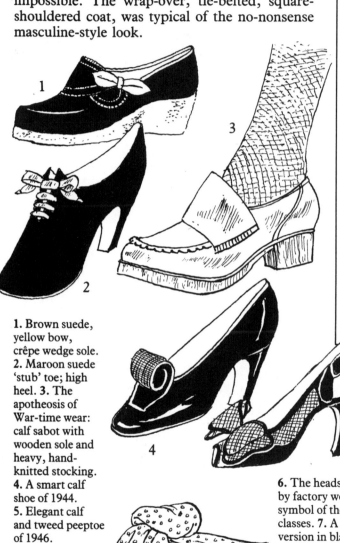

1. Brown suede, yellow bow, crêpe wedge sole. 2. Maroon suede 'stub' toe; high heel. 3. The apotheosis of War-time wear: calf sabot with wooden sole and heavy, hand-knitted stocking. 4. A smart calf shoe of 1944. 5. Elegant calf and tweed peeptoe of 1946.

6. The headscarf turban worn by factory workers became a symbol of the War for all classes. 7. A sophisticated version in black jersey; bag to match.

Two 'demob' shoes: brown leather Derby with rubber sole and grain leather Oxford. Similar shoes and suits were worn throughout the 1950s.

During the War, with so many men in the Armed Forces, fashion virtually stopped. When, in 1945, men were Demobilized ('Demobbed') they were issued with a standard suit, pair of shoes, overcoat and an already 'oldfashioned' trilby.

Because hats were unrationed, fashion went, literally, to the head. **1.** Brown felt and pheasant feather. **2.** Perched circle of red ribbed felt. **3.** Turban of swathed green voile. **4.** 'Coal-heever' in grey felt. **5.** Black chip straw and veil of the late 1940s.

1947–1955

After the liberation of Paris in 1944, fashion saw a minor revival but it was not until Dior launched his New Look in the spring of 1947 that a revolution occurred. He lengthened the skirt and made it full; he nipped in the waist and shoulders sloped – luxurious femininity was back and, by 1950, superbly flattering.

Because many women could not afford the New Look, all kinds of tricks were used on old dresses: added hems, or the skirt lengthened and the 1880s style achieved by a peplum of a different material. Fur collars were added with muff to match.

Heels were high and peep-toes and slingbacks appeared on shoes for all kinds of day, formal and informal wear.
1. Platform sole with slashed sides.
2. Classic court.
3. Ankle straps were very popular; oddly, associated with prostitutes *and* royalty! Although some hats were wide, most were small.
4. Blue felt and long feather. 5. Crushed black velvet beret.

1. Green felt and quill hat with silk scarf and brooch. **2.** Man's 'Chelsea' boot, in suede or leather.

Although it was confined only to the very smart, the early 1950s saw men dressed as 'New Edwardians' – waisted suits with narrow trousers, jackets and short overcoats with velvet collars – and bowlers. For women the early 1950's skirt was 'middy' length.

3. White silk pillbox – classic 1950's shape. **4.** As typical – little arched pale blue felt. **5.** White straw lined with yellow silk. **6.** Ultra-smart, black and white hat and scarf, coarse veil. **7.** Black, white, two shades of brown for bag and scarf. Note long glove for day. **8.** *Svelte* court.

1955–1960

By the mid 1950s, two new silhouettes were fashionable: the 'trapeze' or 'A' line, and the extremely narrow line with a boxy jacket. Chanel's little loose-fitting suits were also highly popular.

Handbags were envelope shaped (*full-length*) or large squares: in black suede. Shoes were slim and fine heeled. **1.** Grained calf. **2.** Coral-red calf.

Hats were fairly close to the head and fanciful. **3.** Pleated white georgette. **4.** Pale yellow fine straw dome. **5.** Concertina turban of black-dotted white organza. **6.** Imaginative beret of light and dark pheasant feathers.

1. 'Briefcase' handbag in grained and smooth dark brown leather. Suede glove and bamboo-handled umbrella.
2. Coach-hide shoulder-bag. 3. Lemon-coloured calf glove.

Country clothes have always been comfortable, practical and restrained – good tweeds, cloth and leather. Head scarves were much worn. The 1950s saw women at the seaside in pants and loose shirts.

8. Red leather beach sandal, white stitching.
9. White leather sandal with punched holes.
10. Huge straw hats were very fashionable.

4. For country town: brown and grey calf. 5. Honey-coloured calf.
6. Tobacco-coloured calf. 7. Pull-on green felt.

Evening jewellery was exotic: falls of diamonds made matching necklace, bracelet and earring. Evening shoes with stiletto heels: **1.** emerald silk, **2.** lilac calf with lilac, green and white fabric toe.

1950's evening dresses were very romantic: crinolines, sleek sheaths and, as here, by the mid-'50s, short, especially for cocktails and theatre. Silks, satins and chiffon in glowing colours, black and white.

Cocktail hats – worn so often with the 'little black' dress, were varied and witty. **3.** Eye-obscuring black feathers. **4.** Plaited cream silk and short veil. **5.** Light drum of white organza with a pink silk rose and green face-covering veil.

Evening handbag of jade green silk embroidered with blue beads.

1960–1970

The 'Swinging Sixties' – the Beatles, Mary Quant, Jean Shrimpton, David Bailey and permissiveness. For men: flamboyant suits, patterned shirts and ties, long hair. For women: above all, the mini skirt. It was introduced in the late 1950s but by the early 1960s was almost universal. In 1964 Courrèges launched his geometric 'space-age' look.

1. The '50s suede Chelsea boot was given a higher heel, made in leather with an elastic gusset – the Beatle boot. **2.** Tan calf with the new narrow, blunt toes. **3.** Black leather and crocodile – the winkle-picker toe. **4.** Formal black calf. **5.** Calf or suede slip-on.

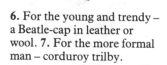

6. For the young and trendy – a Beatle-cap in leather or wool. **7.** For the more formal man – corduroy trilby.

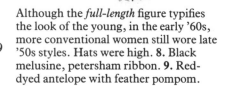

Although the *full-length* figure typifies the look of the young, in the early '60s, more conventional women still wore late '50s styles. Hats were high. **8.** Black melusine, petersham ribbon. **9.** Red-dyed antelope with feather pompom.

1960–1970

With the exposed leg, this was the era of the boot – popularized by Brigitte Bardot – and of the patterned stocking. (Tights were late '60s.)

Full-length. Leather boots – which were often white but also in many light colours.
1. Zipped brown suede. **2.** Longest – in crocodile. **3.** Laced white kid; soft foot. Shoes were shallow: black, white, bright colours.
4. Court. **5.** 'T'-bar sling-back. **6.** Suede sling-back. **7.** Chelsea-style suede boot. **8.** Black leather, metal buckle.

1. Beaded silver lamé sandal; silver stocking. **2.** Dramatic black velvet hood; gilt necklace. **3.** White silk hood with gold balls and braid.

Although long dresses were still fashionable, the mini was popular for evening: often a mere sleeveless tube, often in glittery materials or rich brocade. Large earrings.

In 1964, Courrèges introduced 'space-age' headwear. **9.** Black felt hood with white felt circles. **10.** White felt bound with blue ribbon; bow. The more conventional: **11.** Brown melusine, 'Sherrif' star. **12.** Red and white check cotton pull-on. **13.** The most extreme: black PVC, wired loop.

1970–1980

Men were elegantly formal in (usually single-breasted) suits with narrow waists, wide lapels and – the hall-mark of the 1970s – flared trousers. Informality included polo-necked pullovers and trousers thrust into boots. Hair was still long but, fashionably, very neat.

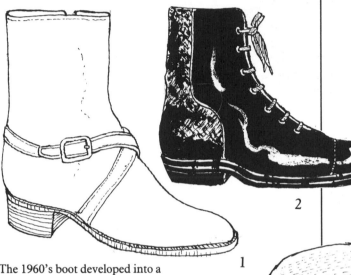

The 1960's boot developed into a longer boot. **1.** In 'cowboy' style, with buckle. **2.** Army-boot fashioned in hard and soft leather. Both: black or tan. Slip-ons were: **3.** in real or fake crocodile or, **4.** in black, tan or maroon leather, with or without tassels.

The Edwardian straw panama hat made a comeback for summer. Patterned and highly coloured ties with large knots were worn with plain or patterned shirts: a fashion which spanned all stratas of society.

Fashion-wise, these were known as the 'uncertain years' – when 'anything goes' was the cry, when skirts ranged in length from just below the knee to the ankle; when the 'ethnic' (or 'peasant') look was fashionable – including knitted wear, padded jackets, bulky coats, full-trousers, blousons, scarves and 'cowboy' boots.

1. Tan leather handbag.
2. Black leather with gilt decoration. Ethnic bags were made of pieces of carpet. **3.** 1920s-style shoe in grey suede, black calf.
4. Cowboy-style boot in orange leather; also in tan or black.

5. Full ethnic: moss suede and cord hat with cream fur brim; bright flower-patterned print wool scarves. **6.** Brown felt pull-on hat, leather band. **7.** Purple and green low-brimmed knitted hat with matching woollen gloves.

Glossary

The dates following each entry indicate when the accessory is illustrated in this book.

Aiglet. 1500–1650. Men and women. Metal tags, often gold or silver and jewelled, with tipped points or ties (resembling shoelaces), or sewn on in pairs as decoration only. *See* Points.

Aigrette. 18th century to 1920s. Women. French for tuft: a spray of feathers or a single feather as a hair or head-dress decoration.

Artois Buckle. 1770–90. Men and women. Extra large shoe buckle.

Babet. 1836–50. Women. Small indoor cap.

Baldrick. 16th century. (Of Medieval origin.) Men. Leather, cloth or velvet sash or band worn round the body from shoulder to hip. 17th century. Similar, buckled and often fringed, to carry the sword.

Baku. 1920–30. Women. Linen-like straw used for cloche hats.

Bavolet. 1830–65. Women. Curtain or frill running around the base of the bonnet at the back.

Béguin. 1500–30. Women. Flemish cap of stiffened lawn or linen. Based on the hood worn by the religious order of Béguins, founded in 1173.

Bergère. 1730–1800. Women. A shallow-crowned, broad brimmed straw hat, also known as a shepherdess (French for this) or milkmaid hat. Revived in the 1870s when it was known as a **Dolly Varden**.

Beret Sleeves. 1820–36. Women. Extra wide sleeves.

Bibi Bonnet. 1830s. Women. Bonnet with compressed angle between crown and brim.

Bicorne. 1770–1810. Men. 19th-century name for a man's hat with a shallow crown and large brim, cocked (turned-up) back and front.

Billiments. 1530–80. Women. Decorative borders for the French hood. Often of jewelled gold or silver, called upper and nether (lower). *See* French Hood.

Bishop's Sleeves. 16th century onwards. Men and women. Full sleeves caught at the wrist with bands.

Bongrace. 1530–1615. Women. An oblong fold of black velvet, square or rounded in front, hanging down the back, worn over the French hood or on its own.

Bowler. 1860s onwards. Men. Hard felt hat with narrow curled brim. Named after a felt-maker, William Bowler. Early 1900s. Women. Worn, with veil, for riding.

Brisé Fan. Oriental origin. Fan made of sticks only, joined by threaded ribbon.

Brogue. 20th century. Men and women. Shoes made of leather in many, often contrasting coloured, sections which are punched and/or have serrated edges.

Brooch. Of very early origin. Any precious and semi-precious, often jewelled or enamelled, pinned ornament. Frequently sewn on to garments or accessories in the 16th and 17th centuries.

Canions. 1670–1700. Men. Fabric thigh-fitting extensions worn from trunk-hose to the knee or just below.

Canons. 1660s. Men. Decorative frills below the knee, worn with patticoat or open breeches.

Capote. 1800–10. Women. Bonnet with small crown and very deep brim obscuring the face.

Caul. 16th century. Men. Close-fitting cap of rich material or hairnet-like cap made of ornamental threads, worn under hats. Women. Similar, but made of threads only, and worn alone or under hats.

Chaperone. 1640–1700. Women. Hood or neckerchief.

Cockade. 18th century onwards. Mainly men. Rosette, frill or spray of ribbon (as opposed to tied bow) decoration on hats; of military origin.

Coif. Early 16th century. Men. Linen, cloth, silk or velvet cap tying under the chin, worn under the hat. Late 16th century. Worn only by lawyers, clerics, etc. 16th and 17th centuries. Women. Similar, usually white and lace-edged worn chiefly indoors or under hats. Late 16th century. Basis of fontange head-dress.

Commode. 1690–1710. Women. The wire frame which supported the fontange.

Copotain. 1560–1610. Men. Hat with tall conical crown, moderate brim.

Cornette. 1816 onwards. Women. Any indoor cap.

Cloche. 1908–33, but principally 1920s. Women. Hat like inverted bell.

Clock. 1500 onwards. (Of Medieval origin.) Men and women. The ankle gusset in a stocking. From c. 1540 often in the form of an inverted triangle of embroidery. Early 16th century often on both sides of stocking; later, on outside only.

Crêpe de Chine. 20th century. Fabric with fine silk warp and tightly twisted worsted weft.

Cuban Heel. Late 19th, early 20th centuries. Men and women. Fairly staight-sided heel.

Cuirasse Bodice. 1875–82. Women. Bodice fitting closely from breast to hips; named after medieval body armour.

Cypress (also Cyprys or Sipers). Chiefly 16th century. Men and women. Cypress is a transparent material of silk or linen, similar to crêpe, smooth or crimped and, when a band, used to decorate hats. Also used for mourning clothes.

Derby Hat. Late 19th century onwards. Men. American word for bowler hat – named after the Epsom race.

Derby Shoe. 20th century. Men. Boot or shoe with eyelet tabs on vamp.

Dolly Varden. 1870s. Women. Straw hat – version of the 18th century bergère.

Enseigne. 1500–50. Men and women. A hat brooch.

Epaulette. 17th century onwards. (Of military origin.) Men and women. Ornamental shoulder-piece.

Falling Band. 1540–1660. Men. Turn-down collar of varying width.

Fichu. 18th and 19th centuries. Women. Silk, lawn, cambric or lace triangular shawl for neck and shoulders.

Filigree. Jewellery. Twisted and soldered thin strands of gold and/or silver wire, forming intricate patterns.

Fob Seals. Late 18th and 19th centuries. Men. **Fob.** The small pocket in the waistband of breeches or trousers from which a chain was hung, decorated with a watch or **seals** – precious or semiprecious metal and semiprecious stones engraved with the owner's crest or monogram. In the 19th century, hung on watchchains.

Fob Watches. 1770–90. Men and Women. Worn in pairs by women, principally in France.

Fontange. 1690–1710/12. Women. Head-dress of several stiff frills of linen and lace supported by the commode and attached to a close-fitting cap. With streamers or lappets.

French Hood. 1530–80. Women. Small curved and stiffened head-dress worn on the back of the head; edged with upper and nether billiments. 1525–58. English version had a straight upper billiment.

Georgette. 1914 onwards. Thin sheer silk fabric with a crêpe effect.

Gores. Of early origin. Men and women. Wedge-shaped pieces of fabric inserted into garments to give width.

Girandole. 18th century onwards. Women. Earring or brooch: three pendants hanging from a top setting.

Grosgrain. 1570 onwards. (Known as 'Grosgram' in the 16th century.) Coarse-grained material of mohair, with silk or worsted.

Halo Bonnet. 1530–50. Men, sometimes women. Hat with small crown concealed by turned-up 'halo'-shaped brim. Usually ornamented with a single ostrich feather and a brooch.

Hessian Boot. Late 18th, early 19th centuries. (Of military origin.) Men. Not named after the fabric – jute or hemp – but after Hesse in Germany. A leather or cloth boot.

High-bodied. 16th to early 17th centuries. Women. A contemporary term for any high-waisted garment.

Homburg. 1870 onwards. Men. Stiff felt hat, dent in crown, braid band around crown, curved brim. So called after Edward VII, when Prince of Wales, who visited Homburg in Germany where the hat was fashionable. He made it popular in England.

IHS (or YHS) Monogram Pendant. 15th to end of 17th centuries. Women. The letters stand for 'Jesus'. Such pendants, made of gold, enamel and precious stones or diamonds were extremely popular throughout Europe among royalty and the upper classes. Usually a breast ornament but small versions were worn on neck ruffs.

Imperatrice. 1860s. Women. Hat named after the Empress Eugenie.

Jabot. Late 19th and 20th centuries. Women. Ornamental frill on bodice; often separate and attached to a collar. Men. Frill on shirt front.

Lappets. 17th to mid-19th centuries. Women. Long streamers hanging from caps or head-dresses, tied, untied or pinned to the top of the head in various ways.

Latchet. 16th and 17th centuries. Men and women. Top fronts of shoes extended into straps or ribbons to tie.

Louis Heel. 18th century onwards. Women. Front surface of heel covered with a downward extension of the sole.

Mule. 1500 onwards. Men and women. Heel-less slipper or slipper-like shoe.

Melusine. 1948 onwards. Women. Long-haired felt, for hats.

Ninon. c.1900 onwards. Lightweight semi-transparent silk.

Organza. Late 19th and 20th centuries. Fine silk fabric of twisted threads.

Ouch. 16th century. Hat brooch.

Oxford Shoe. Late 19th and 20th centuries. Men. Shoes with closed tab.

Paillettes. 16th century onwards. Bright metal disks or spangles.

Panes. 16th to mid-17th centuries. Men and women. Long ribbon-like strips of material set close and parallel, joined above and below or (rarely) open at one end. Lining showed between the panes or was pulled through. Used on many garments, particularly men's trunk-hose.

Pantofle. Known in the 1530s but particularly popular from 1570 to early 17th century. Men. Heel-less overshoe with thick shoe. Outdoors: strong materials. Indoors: as slippers, often with velvet or brocade upper.

Paste. 18th century onwards. Imitation jewellery, usually diamonds.

Periwig. 1660–1720. Men. Long, curled wig; with **Peruke** so-called particularly 1660–85. A *perruquier* was a wigmaker.

Petticoat. Early 16th century. Men. A 'pettie' or small, short coat. 16th to 18th centuries. Women. Panel of material (also called a **Forepart**) inserted between the inverted 'V' of the overskirt. Also, and later, a concealed underskirt.

Petticoat Breeches. 1660s. Men. Breeches with full skirts.

Pinner. 1720–50. Women. Small cap, with or without lappets.

Pinking (also called Pouncing). 16th to early 17th centuries. Men and women. Small holes or slits cut into material, symmetrically arranged to form a pattern; particularly on shoes and men's jerkins. (In the 20th century, **Pinking** is a border cut into angles or scallops – it dates from the second half of the 17th century.)

Points. 1500–1650. Men and women. Pairs of ribbons used to tie one garment to another or a sleeve to the bodice of a garment. Ribbons were threaded through eyelet holes on the other side and tied in a bow. Given ornamental tags called aiglets. Bows of ribbon with aiglets were also used especially in Spain in the 17th century, but for ornament only.

Répoussé. Metal-work in which the design is hammered into relief from the reverse side.

Reticella. Mid-16th to early 17th centuries. Earliest form of handmade needle-point lace. Unlike bobbin lace, made with threads and bobbins (bones) needlepoint is more like embroidery.

Revers. 17th century onwards. Men and women. The turned-back lapels of a coat or jacket.

Round-eared cap. 1730–60. Women. Small cap with single or double frill at the front only, ending at the ears. With or without lappets.

Shadow (also called a Cornet). 1580–1650. Women. Linen or lawn lace-edged cap, rounded in front. Most popular 1605–1620.

Sling-back. 20th century. Women. Shoe with strap around the back of the ankle.

Solitaire. 1720–70. Men. Black silk ribbon neckcloth.

Souvenir Fan. 1870–1910. Wood frame fan with pleated paper circle which is expanded and closed by pulling ribbons. Often with mirror on one side.

Spanish (or Court) Bonnet. 1575–1600. Men. Small-crowned, narrow-brimmed hat, usually of black velvet and decorated with a small plume and jewelled ornament. Worn at backward angle at Court.

Standing Band. 1605–20. Men and women. The **Falling Band** or collar in semi-circular form, made of starched lawn, cambric or lace or lace edged, supported by a wire frame called a Supportasse or Underpropper. For women, also called a **Rebato.**

Stiletto Heel. 1960s onwards. Women. Very thin heel with tiny top piece.

Surah. 19th century onwards. Soft twilled, usually one-coloured, silk, used mainly for hats.

Tassets. 1550–1650. Men and women. The skirts of the doublet or bodice divided into flaps, which sometimes overlapped.

Tippet. 16th century onwards. Women. Fabric or fur small cape or collar.

Tongue. 1500 onwards. Men and women. Shoe or boot: extension of the vamp under the latchets, laces or buttons. Belt: the end which passes through the buckle – the point often ornamented with metal to match the buckle.

Tricorn. 1690–1800. Men. 19th-century name for shallow-crowned hat with brim turned up on three sides: three-cornered hat.

Trilby. 1895 onwards. Men. Soft felt (later, also corduroy) version of the Homburg. Named from the novel of that name by George du Maurier, published 1895.

Trunk Hose. 1550–1610. (Court-wear into the 1620s.) Men. Also called, slops, trunk, upper-stocks breeches, trunks, round or French hose, etc. The upper, or breech garment, extended from waist to hips and was usually paned.

Tulle. Fine net-silk fabric.

Undress. 17th to early 19th centuries (military term for informal uniform for longer period.) Men and women. Informal or casual dress, indoors or early day and late evening.

Venetians. 1570–1620 – most popular 1580–90. Men. Knee breeches. 1570–80s, close-fitting, often worn with cross-garters. 1570–95, wide above, narrowing to knee: pear-shaped. 1570–1620, voluminous and smooth up to 1610, after which heavily pleated.

Virago Sleeves. 1620s. Women. Sleeves, double-ballooned and paned.

Bibliography

Alexander, Hélène *Fans* Batsford, London 1985.

Amphlett, H. *Hats: A History of Fashion Headwear* Richard Sadler, London 1974.

Armstrong, Nancy *Fans: A Collector's Guide*. Souvenir, London, 1984.

Batterbury, Michael & Ariane *Fashion: A Mirror of History* Columbus, London 1982.

Baynes, Ken & Kate *The Shoe Show: British Shoes Since 1790* Crafts Council, London 1979.

Black, J. Anderson & Garland, Madge *A History of Fashion* Orbis, London 1985.

Boehn, Max Von *Modes and Manners* 4 Vols. George Harrap and Dent, London 1909–35.

Blum, Stella *Victorian Fashion & Costume from Harper's Bazzar* Dover, New York 1974.

Brook, Iris *Footwear* Pitman, London 1972.

Buck, Anne *Victorian Costume and Accessories* Herbert Jenkins, London 1961.

Byrde, Penelope *The Male Image: Men's Fashions in Britain, 1300–1970* Batsford, London 1977.

Costume of the Western World:
    Laver, James *Early Tudor*
    Blum, André *The Last Valois*
    Reynolds, Graham *Elizabethan and Jacobean*
    Readem, Brian *The Dominance of Spain*
    Thienen, Frithjof van *The Great Age of Holland*
    Blum, André *The Great Age of Holland*
      George Harrap, London 1951.

Clark, F. *Challenge to Fashion, Gloves 1600–1979* Worthing Museum, 1979.

Courtais, de G. *Women's Headdresses and Hairstyles* Batsford, London 1970.

Cunnington, C. Willet & Phillis *Handbooks of English Costume, Medieval to 19th Century* 4 Vols. Faber, London 1954–1970. *A Picture History of English Costume* Vista, London 1960.

Cunnington, C. Willett *English Women's Clothing in the 19th century* Faber, London 1938. *English Women's Costume in the Present Century* Faber, London 1952.

Davenport, Millia *The Book of Fashion* Crown, New York 1948.

Digby, G. W. *Elizabethan Embroidery* Faber, London 1963.

Dorner, Jane *Fashion in the Twenties & Thirties*, Isa Allen, London 1973

Earl, Alice Morse *Two Centuries of Costume in America 1620–1820* 2 Vols. New York, 1903.

Ewing, Elizabeth *History of Twentieth Century Fashion* (Reprint, Dover, N. Y. 1970) Batsford, London 1973.

Farrell, Jeremy *Umbrellas and Parasols* Batsford, London 1985.

Foster-Harris *The Look of the Old West* Viking, New York 1974.

Glynn, Prudence and Ginsburg, Madeline *In Fashion: Dress in the 20th Century* Allen & Unwin, London 1978.

Harrison, Michael *The History of the Hat* Herbert Jenkins, London 1960.

Holland, Vyvyan *Hand Coloured Fashion Plates, 1770–1899* Batsford, London 1955.

Howell, Georgina *In Vogue – Sixty Years of Celebrities and Fashion from British Vogue* Penguin, London 1978.

Kelly, M. Francis and Schawbe, Randolph *Historic Costume, 1490–1790* Batsford, London 1929.

Kennett, Frances *The Collectors' Book of Twentieth Century Fashion* Granada, London 1983.

Kybalova, Ludmila *The Pictorial Encyclopedia of Fashion* Paul Hamlyn, London 1968.

Laver, James *17th and 18th Century Costume* Victoria & Albert Museum and HMSO, London 1951. Intro: Illustrated Klepper, Erhard, *Costumes Through the Ages*, Thames & Hudson, London 1963.

Laver, James. Intro. *Costume Illustration. The Nineteenth Century* Victoria and Albert Museum, London 1947.

Lens, Bernard *The Exact Dress of the Head, 1725–26* (Reprint) The Costume Society and the Victoria and Albert Museum, London 1970.

Levey, Santana M. *Lace: A History* Victoria and Albert Museum and Maney & Son, London 1983.

Mary, Peter *Collecting Victorian Jewellery* Macgibbon & Kee, London 1970.

McCellan, Elizabeth *History of American Fashion, 1667–1870* Tudor, New York 1969.

Mila, Contini *Fashion from Ancient Egypt to the Present Day* Paul Hamlyn, 1963.

Norris, Herbert *Costume and Fashion. The Tudors. 3 Vols.* Dent, London 1938.

O'Day, Deirdre *Victoian Jewellery* Charles Letts, London 1974.

Probert, Christina *Shoes in Vogue* Thames & Hudson, London 1981.

Redfern, W. B. *Royal and Historic Gloves and Shoes* Methuen, London 1904.

Robinson, Julian *The Golden Age of Style: Art Deco Fashion Illustration* Orbis, London 1976.

Rupert, Jacques *Le Costume* Paris, 1930.

Scarisbrick, Diana *Jewellery* Batsford, London 1984.

Sichel, Marion *Costume References, Medieval to Present Day* 4 Vols. 1984.

Smith, W. W. *Gloves Past and Present* New York, 1918.

Squire, Geoffrey *Dress, Art and Society, 1560–1970* Studio Vista, London 1974.

Sulser, Wilhelm *A Brief History of the Shoe* Hally Schumuseum, Berlin 1958.

Swann, June *Shoes* Batsford, London 1982.

Torrens, D. *Fashion Illustrated: A Review of Women's Dress, 1920–1950* Studio Vista, London 1974.

Vanda, Foste *Bags and Purses* Batsford, London 1982.

Visual History of Costume Series:
Ashford, Jane *16th Century*
Cumming, Valerie *17th Century*
Riberio, Alieen *18th Century*
Vanda, Foste *19th Century* Batsford, London 1986.

Wilcox, R. Turner *The Mode in Footwear* Charles Scribner, New York 1948.

Wilson, Eunice *A History of Shoes in Fashion* Pitman, London 1969.

Yarwood, Doreen *English Costume* Batsford, London 1975.

Books on artists, particularly portrait artists, articles in magazines and artist exhibition catalogues can be very useful. A select list:

Behcerucci, Luisa *Bronzino* Milan, 1954.

Borenau, Radu *Holbein* Murray Sales & Service, London 1977.

Hayes, John *Gainsborough* Phaidon, London 1975.

Kerslake, John *Early Georgian Portraits* 2 Vols. HMSO, London 1977

Kurth, Dr Willi (ed) *Albrecht Durer, Complete Woodcuts* Bonanza Books, New York 1946.

Morse, H. K. *Elizabethan Pageantry* The Studio, 1934.

Paulson, R. *The Art of Hogarth* Phaidon, London 1975.

Pope-Hennessy, John *A Lecture on Nicholas Hilliard* Home & Van Thal, London 1949.

Strong, Roy *Tudor & Jacobean Portraiture* 2 Vols. Routledge and Kegan Paul 1949, and HMSO, London 1969. *The English Icon: Elizabethan & Jacobean Portraiture* Routledge and Kegan Paul, London 1969.

Toskett, B. B. *Collecting Miniatures* The Antique Collectors' Club, Woodbridge 1979.

Walpole Society *The Painter HE: Hans Eworth, Vol II, 1912–13; Marcus Gheeraerts, Vol III, 1914; Portraits by Cornelius Johnson, Vol X, 1921–22.*

Waterhouse, E. K. *Gainsborough* Hulton, London 1958. *Reynolds* Phaidon, London 1973.

Exhibition catalogues

National Gallery
Sir Godfrey Kneller, 1971
Johan Zoffany, 1976
Sir Thomas Lawrence, 1979

The Tate Gallery
Hogarth, 1971
The Age of Charles I, 1972
Thomas Gainsborough, 1980

National Portrait Gallery
Hans Eworth: A Tudor Artist and his Circle, 1965–66
Samuel Cooper and his Contemporaries, 1974
Sir Peter Lely, 1978
Van Dyke in England, 1982
William Dobson, 1983
Polite Society by Arthur Devis, 1712–1787, 1984

Victoria and Albert Museum
Nicholas Hilliard & Isaac Oliver, 1971, reprinted 1974.
Princely Magnificence: Court Jewels of the Renaissance, 1500–1630, 1980
Artists of the Tudor Court: The Portrait Miniature Rediscovered, 1520–1620, 1983
John French: Fashion Photographer, 1984–5.